Birds of the West Coast

Paintings, drawings
and text by
J.F. Lansdowne

Foreword by
S. Dillon Ripley

BIRDS OF THE WEST COAST

Volume One

Houghton Mifflin Company
Boston
1976

Published simultaneously in Canada by
M. F. Feheley Publishers Limited
5 Drumsnab Road, Toronto, Ontario, Canada M4W 3A4

ISBN (U.S.): 0-395-24580-x
ISBN (Canada): 0-919880-03-7

Printed and bound in Italy

For my mother, Edith Lansdowne,
to whose courage, resourcefulness, and unfailing
help I owe any success I have achieved.

Contents

Foreword

Fenwick Lansdowne first came to my attention when I visited the Cornell University Art Gallery in Ithaca, New York to see an exhibit of the art of contemporary bird painters during the International Ornithological Congress in 1962. I was immediately struck by the beauty and delicacy of his work, mostly representations of small perching birds, such as his beloved kinglets. The contained style and quality of his painting reminded me somewhat of Archibald Thorburn, the British painter, who illustrated so many works on birds and mammals in the early years of this century. As I had worked closely with another young bird artist in my years on the faculty at Yale University, Robert Clem, whose hero was Louis Agassiz Fuertes, and whose painting at the time derived something of Fuertes' style, I said to myself, "How fascinating; here are the two finest young bird painters in North America, the style of one reminiscent of Thorburn, the other of Fuertes, perhaps the two finest bird painters of *their* time."

Later I came to see more of Lansdowne's work, at the Kennedy Gallery in New York, then in London, and finally with the appearance of the first of his own books on Canadian birds, *Birds of the Northern Forest*. Still later I persuaded Lansdowne to join with me in a project to paint a bird family of the world, the rails, those delicate, sprightly and elusive creatures of marsh and bog-side. Our association has been one of the happiest, and his paintings seemed subtly to enlarge and emerge into a style of his own as he worked.

Now with this book on the birds of the west coast, he seems to have come truly into his own, a towering figure, at ease, a commanding assurance in the delineation of birds. These are the birds of his own backyard, that marvellous out-of-doors that stretches all round Vancouver Island. He has portrayed them with a superb romantic power. They are as impressive in their way as Audubon's birds were a century and a half ago. I believe that in this book, Lansdowne's bird representation has come of age. His text charmingly mirrors the paintings, giving his own particular style to the description of the habits and occurrence of the species. Would that I too had shared some of his views of these birds, in the solemn vastness of the coastal forests, or the gleaming wave-dashed rocks of the coasts. As you read about them you feel that you are there with him. His sensitivity extends into a welcome feeling for the needs of the species, their conservation and that of the vanishing habitat within which they live, diminished but still awe-inspiring. May this volume bring the art of Fenwick Lansdowne to those many lovers of the art and romance of nature which he represents.

S. Dillon Ripley
Smithsonian Institution
November, 1975

Introduction

This book deals generally with some of the birds found on North America's Pacific coast. Because I grew up with them and know them well, emphasis in this first of two parts is placed on birds of the northwest. The title term "west coast" is rather broad, but it would be cumbersome to define the geographical limits of the book more precisely. However, the following pages include not only birds of the coast itself but birds that are found inland as far as the coast range of mountains. A second volume will adjust the balance by covering other species that live between British Columbia and California.

The magnificent land lying between the mountains and the Pacific is covered by a heavy coniferous cloak, the rain forest. Immense and almost impenetrable, the forest dominates all and extends to the brink of the ocean. A silent place it is, for the most part, with dripping ferns and huge, ancient windfalls that crumble to humus in the dense understorey. There, where salal grows higher than a man, the annual rainfall is scores of inches and in the filtered half-light every surface is greenly clothed in moss or lichen. Few birds sing or call. Invisible and high in the canopy, kinglets flutter and pry, their thin sibilant voices scarcely reaching the ground or rising above the sigh of the wind. Winter wrens, miniscule beings in a world of gigantic scale, pour out their silver cascades in the stillness. The throb of a blue grouse challenge may pulse seasonally through the forest but hardly another sound comes to the ears.

Though the forest covers such a great area the coast has other kinds of country, too. The tideline and rocky shore, the estuaries and mud-flats are distinct environments, all having their special birds. Taken together the different habitats of the Pacific northwest harbour a rich and varied avifauna that, because of the mild climate, diminishes little in species and numbers in winter. In this season other parts of the continent may be locked in a crystalline whiteness, almost without birds, but the west coast has an abundance of life.

The species to be seen change with the season, but due to the easy winters some birds can remain while in other regions harsher weather forces them to leave their summer homes. For instance, the robin that elsewhere is the easterner's herald of spring, stays in the west throughout the year, wandering in flocks through the countryside. Many seabirds are resident. Murres, puffins and their kin nest on the countless islands and spend the non-breeding months offshore while myriad arctic-nesting ducks pass winters along the seaboard from Alaska south. Other waterfowl, surface feeders such as mallards and wigeon, pintails and teal, share the deltas and fields with geese and swans.

Out of the more than three hundred species on the coast it has been difficult to select only fifty-three to represent all. Choice of one meant exclusion of another that would have been equally appropriate. Several birds that appeared in earlier volumes on the northern and eastern forests reappear in this one, partly because they belong here too, and partly, I confess, because I wished to paint them again.

This may be a place to say something of my early interest in birds and painting. The pattern was not unusual; with most naturalists and artists fascination with their subjects takes hold at a young age and so it was with me. I cannot remember a time when I did not draw or when the birds about me were not familiar. Several times while writing the simple biographies for this book I recalled my first acquaintance with the species at hand and realized that it was among my earliest memories. When I was very young—no more than four or five—we lived near Cowichan and Mill

Bay on Vancouver Island. It was there that birds began to attract my attention. I vividly recall the plummeting, erratic nighthawks of summer evenings, the flocks of plaintive waxwings and the great, flame-crested pileated woodpeckers that hammered at the roadside stumps.

The winter of 1942 froze everything in our cottage, even a ruby-crowned kinglet seeking shelter in the woodshed. My mother found it as she went for fuel to feed the range in our orange-floored kitchen, and together we examined the tiny body and brilliant crown. That kinglet may have set the mould for my life's interest. Or perhaps it was already set.

My source of information in those days was the fat, red buckram-bound *Birds of Canada*, by P.A. Taverner. Its brief descriptions, drawings and colour plates gave me endless pleasure. I had not heard of Fuertes nor, indeed, of anyone else, and Allan Brooks' little paintings, so evocative and charming, long remained my standard of excellence in bird painting. The book was a present on my sixth birthday and I came to know it so well that by the time I saw a species in life it was already quite familiar. Many times my poor mother was aroused at dawn to see a waxwing or a towhee or some other avian treasure. She bore it patiently.

I needed no encouragement to draw, though I had lots of it from an artistic and talented parent. In spite of this, some years elapsed before the two almost parallel interests of art and birds converged. Now and then I come across my early drawings or old notebook sketches with their earnest notations of field-marks and sightings. They date from elementary and high school times and seeing them now as the efforts of someone else, I am not sure that I could discern much promise.

I had little instruction in drawing birds. What I did receive was from Frank Beebe at the British Columbia Provincial Museum. For his candid criticism and generosity in sharing what he knew, I owe him a great debt. I took many paintings to him but he never flinched from telling me what was bad or from showing how to make it better.

Each painter develops his own style and approach to his subject, though at first he may emulate the technique of other artists. The heroes of my early painting days were Brooks, Fuertes and Thorburn; much later came my admiration for John James Audubon. I took something from each of them and developed or adapted it in my own way, to fit my own needs. Others do this, too, of course, and I find that some now base their styles on mine. It is easy to recognize one's own painting disguised thinly or not at all and passed off as an original work. At a certain level of competency overt copying should be abandoned and a painter who publishes his work should be able to create his own pictures.

Most bird painters I know use illustration board as a painting surface because of its convenience. I prefer heavy watercolour paper, though it is more trouble to prepare. To me this is outweighed by the more sympathetic quality of the paper and the softer effect it gives to the finished painting.

Descriptions of the way various artists work show that they all differ. Some do almost no preliminary drawing while others give much time and attention to this aspect of their picture-making. I begin with a very rough and slight drawing on scrap paper to give myself a general idea of what I am attempting. The working out of the composition and the position of the figures is done largely on the surface to be painted. Almost always the birds are life-size.

In the matter of scientific names of the birds in this book, I have used only binomials except in a very few instances; that is, I have not indicated either in Latin or English the subspecies depicted or described. When I have been more particular, it is because the subspecies shown is noticeably different in appearance from other races.

This is not a scientific book or one that claims to impart new information to people whose knowledge of the subject is already extensive. Rather it is a volume of paintings, and the short descriptions accompanying the plates are intended to furnish some additional interest to those who enjoy birds but know little of their habits and lives.

Paintings

1 Red-throated Loon

Gavia stellata

Loons are placed near the beginning of bird books because they are considered to be among the more primitive living birds. They are not the oldest but have been around in a recognizable form for a good sixty million years. Loons do look reptilian at times, with sinuous shapes that remind us of the saurian beginning of every avian form. The flightless *Hesperornis* of Paleocene times must have looked very like a loon as it cruised the seas of pre-history.

I know the red-throated loon only as a winter visitor to the waters around my home on Vancouver Island and in this role it is most familiar to people of the west. We see only the speckled plumage of the cold season but others, who spend summers on the tundra, see the striking breeding dress and hear the wild yells and gabblings for which this diver is known.

There is a great migration of red-throated loons along the west coast in spring but little is seen of it; the birds travel high and a mile or two out to sea. From California to British Columbia they move northward to the breeding grounds in Alaska and other parts of the arctic. Many have paired before beginning the journey and so they pass two by two, strung into long broken lines or scattered bunches. Loons are strong fliers: the steady, regular beating of their narrow wings carries them swiftly and tirelessly over long distances.

The first to arrive reach the high latitudes about the middle of May as the ice is breaking and open water appears on the tundra pools. With harsh cries and goose-like honks, they circle over the green, watery land—the "emerald sponge" of one description—as if undecided where to settle.

These loons are plentiful during the short, intense arctic summer. Their grating voices can be heard at all times of the day; even during the brief hours of darkness they call when others are silent. At this time of year red-throated loons are beautifully marked. The triangular throat patches are rich chestnut against pearl grey heads and the glossy dark backs contrast vividly with the glistening white underparts. The very dense feathers of the bellies have a lustrous, satiny appearance as they do in all loons and grebes. (Perhaps this is a form of streamlining to aid in swimming under water.) The archaic-looking ruddy duck has the same quality to the underparts of its body.

When they first come to the northland, loons are garrulous exhibitionists and in the ardour of their courtship they circle and wheel through the air, curving about one another and calling loudly. On the water again, they dive and splash with many exuberant antics, disporting themselves irresponsibly before raising their families.

Two, occasionally three, smooth brown eggs are laid in a nest composed of weeds and grass with a feather or two to serve as lining. The material is dragged up by the billful to form a low hummock on a marshy island or pond edge, never more than a few feet from the water. No attempt is made to disguise the nest and, indeed, in such open country it would be difficult for so large a bird to hide while incubating. A well-worn track is soon beaten smooth by their big webbed feet as they come and go. Their legs are placed far back, so walking is not easy, but on the short journey to the nest they walk almost upright in a penguin-like way. When leaving it is simpler to flop off on their bellies and slide into the water like newly-launched ships.

The chicks at first are covered in a dark brownish down, becoming paler as they grow. While still very young these little loons are accomplished swimmers that follow their parents, take rides on their backs and hide obediently when warned of danger. If the threat is real the old birds resort to diversionary tactics to draw attention away from their babies; these consist of flappings and splashes that are very distracting. The young are slow to mature. The body feathers have grown in and almost all the down has gone before the pinions appear and the birds are able to take to the air. Yet they must be strong on the wing and ready to travel by summer's end, for they can rise only from the water. A loon that has waited too long is trapped and will die on the frozen surface of its home.

The British have a more dignified name for these birds—they call them "divers"—but in North America we have named them "loons" because of their crazy, lunatic laughter. All species make whole orchestras of demented noises that can sound weird enough to raise the hackles on one's neck. Sometimes, though, they are beautiful and appropriate to their setting. For example, much of the magic of the north woods would be missing without the wild, haunting voice of the common loon. So in places where red-throated loons are found, their strange cries are a characteristic and not unpleasant feature of the country.

Loons feed to a large extent on fishes which they capture in swift subaqueous pursuit. Propelled by their large feet (and wings, too, in emergencies) they are fast and manoeuverable enough to outswim their prey. Fishes too large to swallow immediately are brought to the surface and subdued by a few shakes and flips before they slide head first down the long throat.

2 Horned Grebe

Podiceps auritus

A horned grebe in winter bears little resemblance to the puff-headed black, buff and chestnut *exquisite* it becomes in spring. However, to those of us living on the Pacific coast it is the grey and white plumage assumed in the cold months that is more familiar. By then all that remains of the courting and breeding brilliance is the scarlet and yellow eye which A.C. Bent, in his *Life Histories of North American Birds*, described as the most beautiful he had seen in any bird.

Singly or in little groups this grebe spends the winter on the waters of the coast, never far offshore but never coming to land unless oil-soaked or sick. Just beyond the breaking waves, it dives neatly and effortlessly for the small fish and crustaceans that make up its food.

Under water, the horned grebe swims superbly, keeping wings close to the body and using only its well-adapted feet for propulsion. Seldom required for walking, the feet are placed far to the rear and the toes, better than being merely webbed, are lobed in a way that presents a large surface for thrust and barely any to impede the recovery stroke. Dives in search of food last half a minute or more and they are capable of remaining submerged for much longer.

In spring and fall horned grebes migrate, legs trailing, necks drooping, narrow wings beating quickly to keep them airborne. They are strong fliers and as they travel along the coast or through the interior they fly high in ones and twos or little flocks. Audubon wrote of seeing them following the courses of streams on their route.

Breeding takes place on freshwater sloughs and ponds where the grebes build a floating nest of rotting vegetation about a foot in diameter. Lightly anchored to the nearby reeds, the nest is otherwise completely free-floating and after laying is completed, contains four or five eggs. When not incubating, the parents cover the eggs with a few dabs of vegetable matter to hide them, for the nest is quite exposed to view.

The young birds swim and dive almost as soon as they have hatched and dried. At first cryptically marked with light dots and dashes on their black down, they accompany the adults for the remainder of the summer or take free rides on their backs. At this time the food supply is a little more varied and frogs, leeches and all sorts of water insects go down well. Oddly, so do feathers. The stomachs of grebes examined in food studies have contained these in large quantities, but the reason is unknown.

For a long time in childhood, I did not associate the strange broken little cry I would hear offshore with the horned grebe, for it seems to be uttered when the bird is resting far out and not when feeding close to the beach-bound observer. There is a love-song, too, which I have not heard. From what I have read, it seems indescribable, consisting of shrieks, croaks and other loud notes and chatterings that must, I suppose, fall sweetly on the ears of other grebes in the season of love.

3 Brandt's Cormorant

Phalacrocorax penicillatus

Cormorants, snake-necked and reptilian, are so much a feature of the northwest Pacific that it would be hard to imagine that coast without them. They stand on every rocky islet; each buoy and channel marker is a perch for one or two and they can be seen on every waterway.

Brandt's cormorant is the largest and most abundant of the species on the coast. A large, heavy-bodied bird with a bare blue throat or "gular pouch," it ranges between southern Alaska and lower California. Throughout this area it breeds in large colonies, the birds packed so closely together that a visitor sometimes has difficulty stepping between nests. They seem to prefer the sloping sides and tops of rocks to the perpendicular cliff-faces favoured by other species. Although the nests are therefore more accessible to intruders, to reach the island colonies at all is not an easy matter, for ocean swell makes landing difficult.

Brandt's cormorant builds a nest of seaweed, sea moss and eel-grass, diving for and collecting the material in the waters around the colony. Three or four eggs are laid which in due course hatch into blind, naked young. Their black, greasy-looking skins quickly sprout a covering of brownish down and by summer's end they are fully feathered in brown with pale chests and throats. This is the plumage shown in the accompanying painting of a young bird in its first winter that I picked up dead on the beach.

About three years are needed for the adult plumage to become complete, each moult making the bird less brown until the shiny black and filamentous nuptial plumes show that the cormorant is mature.

Those who have visited a cormorant colony will not have forgotten the experience. The thick deposit of droppings whitewashing the rocks, the flies, the overpowering stench of rotting fish and regurgitated food all combine to make it a memorable occasion. The sitting birds are fed by their mates who deposit little piles of fish beside the nests for the hungry incubators.

The food is almost entirely fish and in their searches the cormorants dive to considerable depths. One of A.C. Bent's contributors estimated that they go down as much as a hundred and fifty feet. Sometimes schools of fish come to the surface, perhaps to escape predators below. When this happens the cormorants gather and the surface of the water is covered, sometimes for hundreds of yards, by a seething, flapping mass of black birds. Above them dart the gulls, snatching what they can.

Old-time naturalists were less considerate than modern ornithologists; birds were so numerous fifty to a hundred years ago that it must have seemed no amount of shooting or careless tramping through colonies would deplete them. This is brought to mind when one reads old accounts of days among the birds. In describing an 1895 visit to a California colony, one writer tells of putting all the sitting birds off their nests. He remarks complacently that in the confusion the young became so hopelessly mixed and scrambled that the parents would have had trouble separating them. Two nestlings took refuge on an outlying rock where the waves submerged them at every surge. He does not mention the gulls that swooped onto the unattended nests and destroyed the eggs.

4 Brant

Branta bernicla orientalis

A few feet off the beach, and following its contour, paddle the geese. Lightly balanced in the water and rocking gently as they swim, each of them is an exact and exquisite replica of the others. These are the little sea-going brant that grace one part or another of the whole Pacific seaboard in winter and on migration.

Most commonly, we see them nowadays in bands of one or two hundred where formerly they may have come in thousands, but they are still plentiful and sometimes gather in large flocks a mile or so offshore. In February and March and even into May almost every northwestern beach has a string of brant feeding at the tide-edge or resting on the sand. They are small geese, hardly larger than some of the sea ducks (and lighter than scoters) but they are among the finest-looking waterfowl I know. To someone long ago seduced by the line and form of birds, they ravish the eye with their colouring and trim subtlety of shape. A flotilla of brant, riding alert and buoyant, elegantly necklaced and with white rumps gleaming, is a beautiful sight. Nor is the pleasure merely visual, for the soft, urgent gabbling of their voices as they converse among themselves is as stirring as their appearance is lovely.

Brant have a natural history almost entirely marine, their lives being closely bound up with the sea and what it produces for them in the way of food. In this way they are rather different from some of their relatives such as the Canada geese that spend much of their time on inland fresh water. Brant feed largely on marine vegetation, spend their winters on the salt water and breed on or near the coasts of the far north. Often on their migrations they show a reluctance to cross even narrow points of land, preferring to fly around them in the characteristic wavering lateral lines and leaderless groups. Generally, they fly low over the water but even when high in the air and covering long distances they do not adopt the traditional v-shaped formations of other geese.

Our bird of the Pacific was formerly known as the black brant and was thought to be more or less distinct from the lighter-bellied Atlantic form. It is now accepted that the two kinds are simply different races of the same species. Really, there is no definite line between them and there is much mixing as well as variation of colour in individuals.

For brant geese the single most important source of food is furnished by the great beds of eel-grass that lie in the shallow waters of both the Atlantic and Pacific coasts of America. At low water these beds are partially exposed and easily reached by the geese which come to clip and consume the long green ribbons. Particularly sought are the crisp, white basal parts and roots of the plants; in a party of feeding brant many can be seen tipping up to reach them in the manner of surface ducks. Inevitably, many of the sheared-off eel-grass fronds float away and form loose rafts that later supply the birds with food when the rising tides have put the anchored beds beyond their reach.

Eel-grass is a staple but is not the only food. Brant usually do not seek the tough mussels and other shell-fish favoured by scoters or harlequins; but out of rock crevices and tide-pools they pick little crustaceans and molluscs. Crabs and other animals sheltering in the eel-grass forests must often be devoured along with the greenery.

In high latitudes, on the tundra lakes of Alaska and eastern Siberia, the brant builds a more or less elaborate nest—it depends on the individual—on marshy ground within a downy young's easy reach of water. The nest is a deep, warm bed and blanket of clean down which cushions the three to six eggs and covers them when the incubating parent is away. Some protection from predaceous animals is afforded by the brant's habit of building on little boggy islands rather than on the main shore. Tended only by the female, the nest is guarded vigilantly by the male bird which no doubt is as wary and menacing as any farmyard gander.

Upon hatching, the light-greyish goslings run hastily and almost immediately to the nearest water where for the remainder of summer they feed on a diet of aquatic plants and the rich insect and animal life of tundra lakes. On their first little journey from the nest and also later, they must elude arctic foxes as well as voracious gulls and jaegers that will snatch up a baby brant and bear it away.

In September, like almost all arctic-nesting birds, the brant begin their southward migration. While on the way they seem to stay more on the open sea and so we see fewer of them in the bays and estuaries than in the spring.

These magnificent birds spend the winter months in the hospitable waters of lower California until the renewed urgings of spring bring them beating north along our coast once again.

5 Bufflehead

Bucephala albeola

Among the sea ducks spending the winter in thousands along the coasts of British Columbia and Washington, none is more attractive than the bufflehead. A diminutive (the smallest sea duck), strikingly patterned, and very lively species, it is seen from November till late April in little parties of eight or ten, all splashing and chasing each other in almost constant activity.

Buffleheads, sometimes called "butterballs" because of their fat, solid little forms, dive for their food. They prefer shallow water such as flooded tide flats or the waters just off a beach where they will often feed right in the breakers. As wintering birds on the salt water they eat mainly crustaceans, molluscs, and other small marine invertebrates. Not all members of a feeding party go under at one time. One or two usually remain on the surface to keep watch and should some danger approach, all the birds either dive or take flight with a rapid pattering of pink feet. The length of time under water is about fifteen or twenty seconds and the resting period on the surface somewhat less. If the water is very shallow, then their dives are short and quick.

Wherever there are buffleheads there is a lot of action—wing-flapping, chasing and sudden diving all performed with a jerky, wind-up-toy quality that is enhanced by the birds' small size and the painted appearance of the males. Toward spring much of the activity is due to courtship and sexual rivalry, the drakes at this time making short splashy flights, bobbing their heads in display and seeing off other males. A group engaged in this fashion is a very pretty sight as several drakes, with upward and outward jerks of their puffed-out heads, pursue a single softly-coloured female. She can see what is visible only at close range: the beautiful range of violets and greens on the males' heads. At any distance over a few feet these feathers appear quite black.

Spring migration takes the buffleheads away from the sea and onto the ponds and sloughs of the continent's interior. Here the females lay and brood their six to ten eggs, usually in the abandoned nesting holes of flickers. These cavities are generally quite high up in the dead stubs of soft-wooded trees. In the northern part of the bufflehead's range, a species of poplar is almost always used by the flickers and subsequently by the ducks.

The proximity of water is essential in choosing a nesting site. The ducklings, once they have scrambled up out of the nesting cavity and made the long jump to the ground, should have only a short distance to walk before experiencing their first swim. The longer the distance between tree and water's edge and the more tangled the undergrowth, the more chance of a duckling's becoming lost. Even a brood that reaches the water safely may lose a member or two to a hungry pike, whose sudden snap can make a duckling disappear faster than ever it could dive. As the water must be near, so it must also be shallow to allow successful feeding. The summer diet is much more varied than in winter. All manner of insects are eaten—dragonflies, damsel-flies and beetles being popular in both adult and larval stages. Some plant food is consumed but mostly it is the rich animal life of the ponds that nourishes the little ducks and makes them strong and fat. By September the young birds, looking rather like their mothers, are ready for the southward and outward migration that takes them to the wintering grounds on the Pacific and Atlantic coasts and south.

The bufflehead is not highly sought after as a game bird for it is no great test of a gunner's skill, being conspicuous and rather easy to hit. Nevertheless, in the late nineteenth and early twentieth centuries it suffered greatly from overshooting, and its numbers were seriously reduced. Now, with closed seasons and comparatively stringent bag limits, it is recovering though not yet really abundant in any part of its range.

Some authorities believe that the bufflehead's value lies more in its aesthetic appeal than in sport shooting. Most people who have watched these birds will agree, for their littleness and attractive actions and behaviour make them the most endearing of ducks.

6 Harlequin

Histrionicus histrionicus

On any spring day along the shores of Vancouver Island, little parties of harlequins can be seen. They swim close to the rocks, the bravely-marked drakes jerking back their heads and displaying to soberly-clad, seemingly indifferent females. One often hears the soft clucks and whistles of the courting birds and as sunlight strikes them it picks out the rich chestnut flanks and slaty-blue bodies of these lovely ducks.

"Lords and ladies" is one of their names, at least on the Atlantic coast. It is derived from their elegant, rather bizarre colour pattern, as is the more common "harlequin," coming from the patchwork figure of the Italian comedy. Even the Latin *Histrionicus* refers to the "theatrical," grease-painted look of the males.

Harlequins winter in considerable numbers from Puget Sound north along the coasts of British Columbia and Alaska to the Aleutians. Visiting the latter islands early in the century, A.C. Bent saw "immense flocks" and even today they are very common in the kelp beds and along the rocky shores of the whole Pacific northwest.

Like other sea ducks they get most of their food by diving in rather shallow water for the crustaceans and shell-fish they enjoy. Greatly favoured by harlequins, and other ducks such as scoters, are the big blue mussels which they wrench from vast beds that cover the undersea shelves and ledges. However, this species takes quite a lot of its food on the surface, particularly from around the rocks at low tide when little crabs and other marine animals are exposed.

Less familiar to most people than the wintering harlequin of the coast is the same duck on its breeding grounds. Sometime in April or early May it leaves for the treeless Alaskan islands or goes inland to the fast-running streams and torrents of the mountains. There the female lays her five to ten eggs and, without assistance from her mate, raises the young. A harlequin's nest has been described as being very like that of oldsquaw or eider, that is, built of dried plants and grasses and lined with down plucked from the female's breast. Usually it is on the ground or in a hollow tree stump near water.

No water seems too "white" nor rapids too dangerous for these bold swimmers. They dive and wade in the strongest current, even walking submerged on the gravelly stream beds in the manner of dippers. The downy young bob as lightly as corks and come to no harm in the seething streams.

While the females are busy with their families, the drakes return to salt water where they congregate in kelp beds off the coast. But how different they appear in July and August as they skulk furtively in the weeds! Gone are the vivid colours of winter and spring, replaced by a dull blackish-brown plumage similar to that of the females. This is the "eclipse" plumage assumed by ducks in the northern hemisphere during the summer when the flight feathers are shed. Being unable to fly for several weeks before the new pinions and secondaries grow, the ducks are much more vulnerable to attack and their inconspicuous appearance and subdued behaviour at this time may contribute to their safety. It is not until November that the harlequins are once again resplendent in their lordly stripes and splashes.

7 Surf Scoter

Melanitta perspicillata

Scoters are large, heavy-bodied diving ducks. In the four kinds, males are black, females are brown and all have more or less swollen, lumpy bills with red or yellow markings. Of the three species seen in the west, the surf scoter is to my mind the handsomest, and is my favourite of all wintering waterfowl. The big striking drakes with their large bright bills and white head patches make a fine sight as they ride the deep Pacific swell off some wild rocky coastline.

Surf scoters live on the usual sea duck fare of molluscs and crustaceans, mussels forming a staple food. Scoters are particularly well-equipped for this bivalve diet as they are strong enough and sufficiently stout-billed to wrench the toughest mussel from its mooring.

As their name implies, these ducks feed close along the shore where they handle themselves with ease and assurance in the dangerous crash and drag of the breakers. At the moment waves begin to curl over, their rims showing white lines of foam, the scoters dive neatly through, rising imperturbably behind in the safety of the following troughs.

Though still a very common duck on both sides of the continent, I don't know if we could see today the great numbers that used to throng the seaboards and provide such easy sport to Atlantic gunners. I don't think scoters are regarded as a delicacy here in the west but on the east coast "coot-hunting" has long been a favoured pastime with coot stew being almost as traditional a meal as Boston scrod. Either eastern scoters are more palatable or eastern palates less discriminating, for the birds' diet is likely to render them rather strong eating.

I have read an account (in A.C. Bent's *Life Histories*) of what, even in 1878, must have been an astounding sight. The writer tells of going by kayak to Stewart Island in Alaska and there encountering an immense flock of male surf scoters ringing the shores. He estimated that the birds formed a band from half to three-quarters of a mile deep and ten miles long. The time was August and the ducks would have left their mates to the task of baby-raising while they returned to an idle bachelor life of loafing and moulting. As the kayak approached, the nearest ducks took wing, putting the rest to flight in turn until the whole company rose "with a roar like that of a cataract." The air vibrated as they swept away to sea and safety.

Perhaps we could not see such a thing these days and really, I think no-one now living can have any idea of how many birds, of all kinds, there must have been in the early days of America. Who can imagine seeing near New York three hundred bald eagles, as the Scottish-American naturalist Alexander Wilson did on Gardiner's Island one day early in the last century? Think of the passenger pigeons that obscured the sun for hours as they passed, so many that their droppings fell like hail. Now, even fifty eagles on a west coast beach is a fine thing to see and the pigeons have passed to Eternity.

In late spring surf scoters retire to the most inaccessible spots they can find, going inland to raise their young on the borders of wilderness marshes. The nests are difficult to reach and hard to find being well-concealed under bushes or beneath the low-sweeping branches of trees. The five to nine eggs are incubated by the female alone who also takes full charge of the brood when hatched.

In the fall, parents and young alike return to their wintering grounds on the coast and there, on still days, the most characteristic sound is the tremolo whistle of a surf scoter's wings as it paddles along the surface in take-off.

8 Cooper's Hawk

Accipiter cooperii

All the adjectives that come to mind when one thinks of hawks pertain to this species. Dashing, wild-eyed, a swift and sudden bird-killer of the woods, it is the epitome of "hawk-ness."

The Cooper's hawk was formerly perhaps the commonest of the woodland hawks. Relentless shooting and other direct and indirect acts of persecution have made it less plentiful, but in the early days of this century and before, when all birds were so much more numerous, it was the curse of poultry farmers. They called it "chicken hawk" and with some justice, for a pair or even a single hawk can wreak terrible losses on a chicken coop or pigeon loft. Several birds a day may be lost, snatched away before the very eyes of the desperate owner who finds it no easy matter to kill the marauders, so quick are they. A.C. Bent, writing of the Cooper's hawk, sums up their menace: "It is essentially *the* chicken hawk, so cordially hated by poultry farmers, and is the principal cause of the widespread antipathy toward hawks in general."

Cooper's hawks belong to the group known as "accipiters" which differ in both habit and shape from the broad-winged "soaring" hawks of the plains and the narrow-winged falcons. The present species and its kin are birds of tangled cover; they have short, rounded wings and long tails adapted for sudden spread, quick checking and rapid deceleration. In dense growth or in a maze of branches that would make hunting dangerous for another kind of avian predator, they manoeuvre with ease and safety.

The list of birds and animals captured by Cooper's hawks is broad and comprehensive. Primarily hunters of birds, they take anything from sparrows to the large ruffed and blue grouse. A bird of either sex, even the much smaller male, will not hesitate to tackle prey much heavier than itself. Surprise is an important element in the success of the hunt and these hawks take full advantage of bushes and other cover to mask their approach. Their sudden appearance over a hedge or around a tree throws all into panic, allowing the prey little chance of escape. In addition to birds, mammals up to the size of hares and skunks are caught as well as a few frogs, reptiles and even insects in hard times or for quick snacks.

As with the smaller but similar sharp-shinned hawk and the much larger goshawk, juvenile Cooper's hawks are brown above, striped below with lanceolate dark markings on white or creamy underparts. This handsome sub-adult plumage, shown in the painting, is worn throughout the birds' first winter, and in the spring of their second year they begin to breed while still wearing it. A summer moult in the second year produces the slaty back and rusty, transverse barring of the adults. The strongly banded tail is a feature of birds both young and old.

Cooper's hawks build bulky stick and twig nests lined with chips of bark and a few green sprigs. The height from ground level varies, but is generally thirty feet or more. They seem to prefer a new nest each year and both members of a pair bring material and help with the construction. Frequently, however, old nests are repaired or at least used as bases for new ones, and occasionally a crow's or a squirrel's nest is taken over and refurbished.

Four eggs are laid, generally in May, and the chicks, like those of other raptorial birds, are covered in whitish down, short at first and later long and woolly. Through this down grows the new plumage, gradually replacing it. By the time the chicks leave the nest, clambering and flapping on the nearby branches, only a few tufts adhere to their heads marking the passage of their babyhood.

The breeding range of this hawk covers most of the continent and in the west extends well into northern British Columbia. The winter range is a little more restricted and there is something of a fall migration south along the coast. Many of these birds of passage travel along the sea coast and at this time of year it is usual to see Cooper's hawks and sharp-shins, striped juveniles for the most part, flitting along beaches in their "flap, flap, flap—sail" flight so characteristic of accipitrine hawks.

The Cooper's hawk is one of several species commonly kept by falconers, who are wistfully harking back to a bygone time of romantic death. To keep and fly a hawk is absorbing and instructive—it gets into the blood. One must spend a great deal of time with the bird, especially at first, and the intimacy which derives from a close association with such a wild creature can be deeply rewarding. But the indiscriminate taking and raising of young birds of prey by eager, ignorant aspirants to the ancient business of jesses and bells is to be discouraged. It is an old art and full of mysteries but the time for it really is past. There are too few birds now and none to spare for this form of nostalgia.

9 Red-tailed Hawk

Buteo jamaicensis

It could be said that the red-tailed hawk is not particularly a species of the west coast, for it has a distribution that spans almost the entire continent of North America. It is as much at home amid the hardwoods of the east as it is on the prairies or in the desert landscape of the southwest, while above the coniferous forests of the west coast its blunt, circling shape is a familiar sight.

Like other members of the genus *Buteo*, the red-tail's physical structure is adapted to prolonged periods of soaring flight, during which it scans the ground for prey. Making use of rising currents of warm air, it employs its wide wing and tail surfaces to sail with minimum effort in slow circles, rising until it is merely a speck in the sky, if visible at all. Even from great heights it can clearly see any movement of mouse, ground squirrel or snake and with a single whistling dive it descends, braking at ground level to seize its prey.

Hunting from on high is the most dramatic method used by red-tails, but there are others. While perched and apparently resting they are by no means unwatchful; to the contrary, they are alert and ready to pounce at the smallest movement about them.

In different parts of its range there is a good deal of variation in the colouring and darkness of red-tailed hawks, those of desert regions being pale while eastern birds are of a more reddish hue than the western race. In addition, there are in the west light and dark phases, birds of the latter having the browns very deep and the light areas much restricted. However, whether melanistic, or of pale colouring or of whatever phase or shade, the adult hawk has a brick-red tail, usually barred to some extent with black and tipped with white. The young birds are not so easily identified, for the tails are heavily barred brown and in certain parts of the country where other buteos occur, they might give an observer some cause for thought.

Red-tails build the usual raptor nest, a bushy mass of finger-thick branches and smaller twigs that is lined with bark, lichen and bits of greenery. As a general rule, these birds would rather prepare a new nest each season than repair an old one but where there is not a wide choice of suitable places to build, they may resort to the same site for several years. The nest is placed between thirty and eighty feet up in a tree, the kind depending upon what species is common in the district. In heavily-timbered country probably a conifer will be chosen while on the plains it may be an aspen or an old willow; red-tails adapt themselves to the terrain in which they live. In arid, treeless places they raise their broods on bluffs, in shallow, cliff-side caves and even on giant cacti.

Predominently hunters of small mammals, red-tailed hawks feed upon the species most easily obtained. Mice, squirrels, chipmunks and in the open west, gophers and ground squirrels are their usual victims. Should there be somewhere a plague of field voles or other rodents, the red-tails will materialize together with the other "professional mousers," the marsh hawks and short-eared owls.

As a rule, three or four eggs are laid at intervals with incubation beginning before the clutch is complete. This is common with birds of prey and, of course, results in the first-laid eggs hatching before the last. Consequently, well-grown chicks share the nest with the newly-hatched and the latter often suffer death from starvation, crowding or just plain bullying. The incubation period is about twenty-eight days and a further four weeks is needed in the nest before the chicks begin their first uncertain flight.

Adults must spend all the daylight hours hunting to feed even two voracious red-tailed babies. The chicks probably consume their own weight each day in small mammals, birds and snakes. When they are half-grown this is roughly equivalent to half-a-dozen ground squirrels with a few other little animals added as snacks and "extras." The great benefit to a farmer in having a pair of red-tailed hawks living on his land can be easily seen.

Much of the young birds' hunting ability is taught by the parents who patiently mark down easy-to-catch prey for their inexperienced offspring and generally instruct them in how to be successful red-tailed hawks. As soon as the young can fend for themselves the family group disperses.

From the northern part of their range the red-tails migrate in fall, travelling sometimes in flocks or in scattered groups that present marvellous spectacles. This is particularly so in the east where impressive hawk migrations, of several species, take place annually. A clear, cold day with a favourable wind may bring dozens or hundreds of buteos slowly cartwheeling across the sky. One group passes and another comes into view, the individuals riding the thermals, rolling and diving from one column of air to another or ascending into invisibility. On our western coast, where most land bird migrations are less sharply defined, I have not seen red-tails moving south in groups, although when travelling through the interior they may. Our only comparable sights to the eastern hawk migrations are the great flights of turkey vultures that pass by each September.

10 Bald Eagle

Haliaeetus leucocephalus

The last stronghold of the bald eagle is the northwestern coast of America where it still lives in relatively undisturbed abundance. A traveller on the ferries that ply the inside passages between Vancouver Island and the mainland is almost sure to see several during his journey. Farther north in the more isolated, wild parts of British Columbia and Alaska bald eagles are even more numerous, as they used to be throughout their extensive range. Indiscriminate shooting and lately, pesticides, have taken heavy toll elsewhere but here it is not uncommon to see fifty or more. To eastern visitors such sights are like glimpses into the past.

The bald eagle is the national emblem of the United States and it is easy to see how a bird of such fierce and noble aspect came to be chosen. Unfortunately, it does not always live up to the honour, for it is not nearly so dashing or martial a character as the golden eagle. It scavenges and feeds on dead fish and will even shoulder vultures out of the way to take over their feast. However, a bald eagle can and frequently does catch live prey in as fine a style as could be wished. In doing research for this description, I was surprised to read the list of animals that at one time or another have made a meal for an eagle. Almost every living thing from a frog to a deer has been captured.

On the west coast eagles take many ducks and seabirds. These are captured either in direct pursuit or by being harried to exhaustion, forced to dive repeatedly until no strength is left to avoid the great yellow feet of the tormentor. When the salmon run up the streams and rivers to spawn, bald eagles, in company with gulls, ravens and bears, gather to feed on the spawned-out, dying fish. This is the time to see great congregations because as long as the supply lasts, the eagles stay.

At the mouth of the Big Qualicum River, in the brilliant light of a hoar-frosted winter day, I saw such a gathering of eagles. A hundred or so had come to glut themselves on the thousands of dead salmon washed down from the spawning grounds. Fish that once had been an angler's dream lay in rotting heaps; they covered the sands of the estuary, they filled every tide-pool and depression and they were banked up behind logs and stream-side bushes. Everywhere slow, magnificent eagles flapped and wheeled low over the beach and foreshore. Others rested, statuesque and replete, on a row of piles, on rocks and on nearby trees. About eighty stood shoulder to shoulder on a narrow sandbar, shuffling and raising their great wings in petty quarrels. From high overhead, newcomers dropped down to join them. The hundreds of gulls that crowded the beach or rode in great rafts offshore accentuated the size of the eagles and made them appear, by contrast with the smaller birds' whiteness, starkly black.

The huge structures of sticks and branches that are the nests of bald eagles are often built on broken tops of firs or other trees and are very conspicuous. In rugged terrain where trees are stunted or absent, as on a bleak, wind-blown coastline, the eagles will build on rocky ledges, on cliffs and even in caves. Nests are used repeatedly for many years, a new layer of sticks and a fresh lining being added each season. At many old sites the piles are eight or ten or even twenty feet deep and at least six feet across. Earth and pieces of turf together with animal remains and old linings form a solid core that eventually weighs several hundred pounds.

Other creatures sometimes nest in the lower levels of these large ramparts—wood rats, perhaps, or great horned owls. The owls quite often take over abandoned nests but occasionally they cannot wait for a vacancy and will burrow into the sides while the penthouse is still occupied.

Bald eagles seldom, if ever, attack human intruders at the nest but they strongly object to being disturbed. Climbing to the nests and flying over them in small planes or helicopters almost always causes desertion and the birds may not breed again for a year or more. A retired gentleman with an interest in eagles once climbed and investigated just about every nesting tree in Florida; he thereby unwittingly contributed to the decimation of breeding eagles in that state.

Of the two eaglets hatched, sometimes it is only the larger and stronger that survives. It takes the food by main force and the smaller nestling, starved and bullied, becomes weaker and weaker, until eventually it dies and is trampled into the fabric of the nursery.

The bird depicted opposite is immature, perhaps two years old; not for three or four years does a bald eagle assume the white head and tail of the fully adult bird. At nest-leaving time the plumage of the juvenile is a dark brown with irregular white patches showing at the base of some feathers. In the second year much more white appears on the undersides and tail while the feathers of the nape are strongly tipped with light straw colour.

The term "bald" has puzzled those who can see that this eagle is plainly as well-feathered about the head as most birds; however, the explanation is that the word has been retained in its archaic sense, meaning "white-headed."

11 Sooty Grouse

Dendragapus obscurus fuliginosus

"Blue grouse" is the name given generally to a group of large, slaty grouse that in one racial form or another inhabits the forests of the west. The bird that lives in the humid forests of the coast is the sooty grouse, large and dark with a grey band on its tail. At times it is considered either a full species or a race of the others.

I recall so well seeing my first sooty grouse, a fine male lying limp and magnificent in the hand of a Cowichan neighbour. When the feathers of the neck—startlingly white at the base—were parted, the bright yellow air sacs were exposed. Bumpy and deeply corrugated, the bare skin reminded me of corn kernels. Over each eye grew a fleshy comb, also of corn yellow. The size and beauty of that bird impressed my young mind and still comes back to me now.

Sooty grouse are among the most characteristic inhabitants of the coniferous forest from northern California to Alaska. To a considerable extent they are dependent upon the Douglas firs and spend much of their lives in the upper strata of these trees. High in the canopy of interlacing branches they feed and socialize and roost, so quiet and unobtrusive that only the keenest eyes may discern them.

In cold weather the lives of the sooty grouse become entirely arboreal. They remain aloft, fifty or sixty feet above the ground, hardly ever descending to the forest floor. Here in the heavy timber of the upper elevations is found all they need in the way of water, food and protection, for the cover is dense, the rainfall heavy and nourishment plentiful in the form of buds and fir needles. In early March there is a general move down to the more open canyon-sides in the foothills and from there to the low valley-bottoms where in summer the young will be raised. Now the grouse feed on the ground and seem more numerous because they are more easily seen.

In March, too, begins the resonant hooting that is so much a part of spring on the coast. This is the love song of the sooty grouse and its challenge to rivals. Usually delivered from a high perch in a fir, it starts with a series of very low notes, five or six in a sequence. These have tremendous carrying power and can be heard clearly for three or four miles, though when uttered close at hand the calls do not seem especially loud. The source is difficult to locate, seeming to come first from one direction and then another, now loud, now faint.

For those people interested in the technical side of grouse music, the sounds have been described as being "among the lowest tones of Nature's thorobase [sic], being usually about C of the First Octave, but ranging from E Flat down to B Flat of the Contra Octave."

Once discovered, the performer is worth watching. His body tips forward as he droops his wings and raises his spread tail. As he puffs the feathers of his throat and neck, a white rosette, caused by the turning back of the feathers, appears on either side. The yellow air sacs swell and show momentarily in the centre of the rosettes as the notes are forced from the half-open bill. The challenge is issued again and again with a few seconds' interval during which the bird struts hopefully up and down his branch. He responds eagerly to the chicken-like, cackling call of the female.

Sooty grouse nest in dry woodlands, sometimes in quite open situations. A depression is scraped in the earth under a fallen branch or log or at the base of a tree. In the casual lining of debris and feathers six to ten eggs are laid and incubated by the mother. As soon as this is accomplished the males go off in little bands. They pass an agreeably idle summer among the bushes of wild raspberries and other fruit before rejoining their families in the fall.

The chicks stay close for the first two weeks and then, a little stronger and safer, they wander with their parents to the willow thickets along the stream beds. Like the young of other gallinaceous birds, sooty grouse chicks quickly grow serviceable wing feathers and are able to fly before they are half-grown.

The young grouse catch insects and also eat tender plants. As the many kinds of wild fruits ripen they are sought eagerly by both young birds and old. Perhaps the adults are a little tired of fir buds and needles for by this time, late summer, they devour the leaves of plants and also the blossoms of columbine, Indian paintbrush and others.

The sooty grouse is a game bird and has suffered. It is large, weighing three or four pounds, and the summer diet makes it fat and thus very good eating. However, on the winter fare of fir it takes on a resinous flavour and becomes less desirable for the menu.

12 Ruffed Grouse

Bonasa umbellus

The magnificent ruffed grouse must be one of the best known of North America's upland birds. Other species are popular, too, but this is a favourite, both for beauty and sport. In the New England states and parts of Canada it is king, traditionally the hunter's wiliest adversary.

With its wide distribution, the ruffed grouse is plentiful on the west coast but here the vegetation forms cover so thick that it is impossible to see more than a few feet. In such closed surroundings neither bird nor hunter is able to exhibit his skill to much advantage and so the ruffed grouse enjoys less of a reputation with sportsmen than it does elsewhere. It is a woodland inhabitant, frequenting swampy bottoms, alder and aspen woods and other treed places near water. On the coast it comes sometimes into the new growth that springs up on cut-over slash. Many a person has been startled by one of these birds erupting at his feet, a feathered explosion that bursts upward with a roar of wings and planes away.

Among the races found in different parts of the continent are some that are browner or paler than others but all show a marked dichromatism. This phenomenon, noticeably manifest in eastern screech owls too, causes the ruffed grouse to be either basically rufous with orange-red tails or greyish-brown with grey tails. Though the red phase predominates in the east, the colouring has nothing to do with geography, age or sex; birds of one or other phase may be hatched from the same clutch. In some the usually black, green-glossed feathers of the ruff are reddish-brown with copper lights, while the sub-terminal band on the tail may be chestnut.

The ruffed grouse, which bears in some places the old names of "partridge" or "pheasant," was first noticed by European naturalists in the seventeenth century. It attracted their attention chiefly because of its remarkable drumming in spring: mounting a fallen log or some other eminence, the cock grouse beats an astonishing tattoo upon the air, sending the thunder of his challenge a mile or more across woods and hills. It begins with slow, deep claps and builds to a reverberating drum roll that ends as it began.

Until motion pictures established its mechanics, controversy existed as to the way the sound was produced. At first, it was thought to be caused by the beating of wings against the body and later, by wings striking together over the back. Now it is understood that forward and upward strokes of the wings against the air cause the loud drumming that is such a feature of the spring woods. During the performance the bird's body is held vertically while the backward thrust given by the beating wings presses the spread tail flat against the log in a sort of involuntary bracing action.

In addition, the male has a visual display, more for the benefit of his prospective mate. In its way it is equally impressive: he droops his wings and at the same time raises and spreads his tail in turkey fashion. His head crest lifts and the soft-edged feathers of his ruff are raised to form a great, standing collar that completely encircles his neck. In a lateral version of this display, the male turns sideways to the object of his ardour and lifts the off-side of his body so that as much back, side and tail as possible can be seen. The head and ruff are turned toward the female. He struts and bobs, shaking his head until the ruff seems to rotate.

The nest is on the ground and is no more than a slight depression scraped in the earth and sparingly lined with grass and leaves. It is well concealed in heavy cover or under fallen branches and is usually placed at the base of a tree. When the intricately patterned body of the brooding hen has settled on the eggs, nest and mother are virtually invisible.

A dozen eggs, more or less, are laid and as many as fifteen or twenty have been found, though perhaps from more than one hen. Incubation and the care of the young usually is solely the responsibility of the female, for in summer the males go off for a few easy weeks of bachelor living. During this time the chicks are zealously protected by their mother who will attack any intruder, hissing and mewing as she pecks and flies at him. The babies grow quickly and in fall when they are rejoined by the male, the tiny wood-coloured downies have become rangy, full-sized grouse.

Their food is about ninety per cent vegetable. In late summer and fall many kinds of wild fruit ripen and these are all eaten, as are the buds of trees a little later. The buds of apple, pear and other fruit trees are favoured in areas where there are old orchards—the grouse sit around in the branches like the proverbial partridges, picking every bud within reach. Where these delicacies are not available, grouse resort to other trees, not for buds only but for the leaves as well. Insects make up the comparatively small amount of animal food and are eaten particularly by the growing chicks.

In winter, when snow is deep, the feet of these and other species of grouse grow scales that extend laterally from the toes, looking rather like stubby fir needles. These act as snowshoes and aid the wearers in walking on the soft crust.

13 California Quail

Lophortyx californicus

This quail is not a native of the Pacific northwest. However, since its introduction over a hundred years ago, countless generations of the handsome "California partridge" have made their home there and now they are a welcome and accepted part of the local avifauna. Originally they were restricted to California and southwestern Oregon but the range has extended, with the aid of man, and now the California quail occurs north through Washington to the coast of British Columbia and east to Nevada, Utah and Idaho.

This is one of the few introductions that I do not regret, for its presence has done no visible harm. Rather, the quail has enhanced the areas that it has taken for its own and the interference by man was, in a way, no more than a nudge northward to a scarcely alien land. On Vancouver Island, where my acquaintance with them was formed, California quail are the neighbours of man; they live in shy proximity, coming close yet remaining aloof and somewhat wild. Numbers reside on the fringes of towns and in Victoria they are most common in the older residential districts where trees and shrubbery are plentiful, the gardens large and interspersed with wild patches, wooded gullies and parks. Little coveys feeding on the boulevards or racing on blurred legs across roads are an everyday sight. To some extent, seeing them often may dull appreciation of their beauty, for beautiful they are, having an exotic air and most elaborate, delicately drawn patterns and colouring. The amazing plume of dark feathers that springs from the crown is one of the finest and most expressive pieces of bird ornamentation I know.

These birds are plentiful throughout their original home but formerly their numbers were enormous. The market-hunting years saw hundreds of thousands slaughtered for the table—the flocks in the countryside being so great that it was easy to kill a dozen or two with a single discharge of the gun. I believe they are considered game birds still, though their preference for running rather than flying may make them less interesting in this regard. Most hunters like to give themselves a trickier shot and the game a "sporting" chance before they blast it.

California quail usually take to the trees at night but though they roost aloft, they nest as other gallinaceous birds do, on the ground. A dozen or more creamy, dark-spotted eggs are laid in a shallow depression sparingly lined with grass. The protective shelter of a low-hanging bush or the lee side of a log is sought but otherwise the eggs are concealed more by the body of the incubating hen than by any artifice. Three weeks are required for chicks to hatch, then the nest is needed no longer, for they leave at once to follow their solicitous and cautious parents. Responding to the adults' calls at the first intimation of danger, the chicks hide and are next to impossible to discover. One is much more likely to trample them than to find them. The young are able to fly when only half-grown, giving them an added measure of safety and protection from predators.

At this time the male mounts guard on some elevated post, periodically uttering a loud, single-note call to indicate that all is well. Below him in the shrubbery can be heard the rapid *tsk tsk tsk tsk* of the hen as she seeks to keep her brood together. In fall and winter the families merge into flocks and then, too, the males stand picket duty. One sentinel, a bird that has previously checked the ground, stands watch as the flock feeds. As the other members pass beyond him, another male takes up the watch and the first rejoins the group.

There is no migration and quail remain in much the same place winter and summer. They come readily to grain put out for them, for almost all their food consists of seeds with a small amount of other vegetable and a little animal matter. If food is put in a certain place at regular times of the day the quail soon become used to appearing at the appointed hour, thereby giving much pleasure to those who feed them.

14 Black Oystercatcher

Haematopus bachmani

Anyone seeing a black oystercatcher for the first time might be inclined to laugh at its grotesque and rather comic appearance. Its outsized red bill is impossibly bright, the white eyes are red-ringed and the pallid, fleshy feet bring to mind a seaside bather who has taken off his shoes and socks. When the bird nods and utters a piercingly loud whinny, the observer is convinced that it is simple as well as strange-looking.

This is one of several species of oystercatcher, and is the only all-black member in a family of pied birds. It makes its home on the multitude of little islets and outcroppings of rock that lie along the foggy northwestern edge of the American continent. Against the dark-hued rocks the value of the black oystercatcher's uniform colouring becomes apparent. Placed on this background it simply disappears and although there may be several about, it takes some keen searching to discover them even when their shrill calls fill the air.

A little observation also reveals the utility of the long flattened bill with which an oystercatcher pries and probes in its search for food. Tong-like mandibles reach into the narrowest fissures to extract little marine animals hiding there; they are powerful enough to crack a limpet or dislodge a barnacle and can render a mussel helpless by shearing its valve-closing mechanism.

Some of these well-protected shell-fish, such as barnacles, require patience to open and the oystercatchers, rather as crows and jays do, take them to a favourite spot where they hammer the shells apart on an anvil of rock. These breaking places are often surrounded by middens of shattered, discarded fragments. The feet, too, are specially adapted for life in slippery places. An arrangement of surface-gripping pectinations on the toes enables the oystercatchers to traverse the steepest slopes quite safely.

In spring the courtship of the black oystercatchers is interesting to watch, for they go through a lot of neck-stretching and bowing to an accompaniment of whistles and other noises. I cannot find much about it in the literature, and perhaps no one yet has studied it very closely, but likely it would be found that, just like other birds, they use gestures in their love rituals that began as everyday actions. I have seen these oystercatchers engage in what I think was a kind of courtship flight. Unlike their usual rather laboured progress, this was a fast, erratic chase, the two participants flying now high, now low, over the water for several minutes, crying continuously.

Once the choice of partners has been made, the pairs set about housekeeping in a very simple and spartan way. A nest is made by scraping out a two-inch deep hollow which may be lined with shell fragments or chips of stone. Most nests are quite bare, but occasionally a bird will add a grass lining before laying her two or three eggs. These are blotched and spotted so that they are very difficult to see, especially if they lie in a nest built on a shingle beach.

The little oystercatchers are quite charming after they hatch and begin to follow their parents over the rough terrain of their home. Frizzy, small in body but long in the legs, they dart about jerkily and squat instantly on hearing the elder bird's alarm note, becoming invisible in their dark brindled down. They very soon start pecking and chipping at the barnacles, but at first they are not strong enough to make much impression.

There is nothing that could be called a real migration in the lives of black oystercatchers. A shifting about or dispersal of individual birds may take place, particularly after the breeding season but, for the most part, they are residents throughout their range.

J.F. LANSDOWNE
·1973·

15 Black Turnstone

Arenaria melanocephala

What would the weed-strewn shores of the west coast be without black turnstones? Their dark forms creeping and pattering over the tide-edge, the constant trill of their voices and the flash of their wing patterns are an integral part of the coastal scene.

Peculiar to the north Pacific, these chocolate and white birds are dusky counterparts of that gaudy harlequin, the ruddy turnstone, of North America's other shores. The breeding plumage shows, in its white markings and liberal splashing of dots, the distinctive body pattern of the ruddy turnstone, indicating the close relationship between the two species.

Like many other shorebirds, black turnstones breed on the arctic tundra, arriving in Alaska with the earliest spring migrants while ice borders the shore and ponds of thawing snow still stand as the only open water. This is the time of courtship, a noisy period of wild pursuits between the sexes and of the males' solo courtship flights. In the latter, the suitors break down female resistance by circling higher and higher until lost to human view, producing as they again descend to earth a hollow woodwind note. This is similar to the sound made by the stiffly-spread tail feathers of a "drumming" snipe.

Four eggs are laid flat on the ground in a barely perceptible scrape made close to the water's edge. The young of waders are precocious, downy when hatched and able as soon as dry to run and feed with their parents. Turnstone chicks, in blackish brown and cream, are not exceptions; picking and dabbing along the shore for insects, crustaceans and molluscs, they grow quickly and fledge in time to accompany the older birds southward as winter locks the northland.

The first southbound migrants appear on the coast in late July. While it is still summer we may walk the beach and hear the rapid chittering of a little party of early turnstones, the first of the great shorebird migration that sweeps south from the breeding grounds of the high arctic. By early winter black turnstones are everywhere, the commonest waders in the northwest.

These birds favour not so much the strand but rather broken knobs of rock and the little islands and islets that lie just offshore. Where the surging tide hisses into the fissures and crevices, swamping the rock-pools at every lift of the Pacific swell, where in rough weather breakers shatter and spray, turnstones are at home, prying and clambering over barnacles and tangled drifts of weed. Chunky and pigeon-like in shape, with short, stout bills, turnstones are well-adapted to the lives they lead and blend so well with their surroundings that they are all but invisible until they fly. They feed on the countless marine animals that cling to the rocks, burrow in the sand or seek sanctuary in the tide-pools. After an especially stormy night, I see them sometimes on the boulevards and grass of a little seaside park near my home. Looking more like pigeons than ever, they run and peck at the cast-up spindrift, a few feet from passing cars.

Turnstones frequently consort with surfbirds and Aleutian sandpipers, two species that bear a superficial resemblance to them and which share the same barren habitat. These three, all the colour of dark, wet rock, may be seen in the northwest on any winter day, working over the shore or waiting in little groups for the tide to change.

J.F. LANSDOWNE
1975

16 Greater Yellowlegs

Tringa melanoleucus

There is little difficulty in distinguishing this bird from most other shorebirds except the slightly smaller lesser yellowlegs. It does not vex us with hard-to-see leg colour or uncertain identity as do the restless hordes of nearly indistinguishable little "peeps." The legs are so yellow and long that even an inexperienced observer knows, when looking at this species, that he is seeing one of the "yellowshanks." Fortunately for his peace of mind, the lesser prefers to travel an inland route, while in the west the greater yellowlegs favours the coast.

On their spring migration these leggy waders begin to appear on our beaches in late March and April. Alone or in small scattered parties—seldom as many as a dozen—they step delicately over the pebbles and sand with a characteristic bobbing, teetering gait. They swim readily and well, looking like big phalaropes, and often feed while wading up to their bellies in the water. Yellowlegs are fond of minnows and other little fishes which they pursue through the shallows, their heads darting rapidly from side to side. A caught fish is flipped and manoeuvred down the slender bill until it can be swallowed head first. One gulp and it's gone.

By sometime in May most of the breeding birds have reached their nesting grounds. These are among the myriad sloughs and muskeg ponds that lie from northern British Columbia to the arctic tundra. At this time of year, before nesting begins, the long northern days are loud with the plaintive, repetitive song of courting yellowlegs. The males perform endless display flights, spiralling higher and higher until hardly visible while their love song comes down to the earth-bound listener: *teda teda teda*. They stand poised with quivering wings raised and run around the females, whistling continuously.

The nest is always close to water, on a dry ridge or little patch of peat. It is extremely hard to find, for the female when sitting is well-camouflaged and the nest is nothing more than a scrape.

An intruder in the general vicinity is met by the vociferous, screaming male bird while still at some distance from the nest. He does not wait for a close approach but perches in awkward agitation on bushes and trees or flies distractedly about the visitor's head, shrieking.

Four eggs are laid in the scratched-out, shallow depression that serves as a nest. The downy young stay in the nest for about a day after hatching but by the second they have gained sufficient strength to follow the parent around on oversized, uncertain legs. They never return to the nest that is inhabited for so short a time. If they survive the vicissitudes of a small shorebird's life, by late summer they are ready to make the journey to South America.

Yellowlegs are wary birds and in the days when all the large waders were fair game their watchfulness earned them the enmity of many a gunner. They are not called tattlers for nothing—at the first intimation of danger their loud *teu teu teu* alerts every creature within earshot.

17 Dunlin
Calidris alpina

Twice each year hordes of wading birds sweep the coasts of America, going northward in spring, southward every fall. The distances they travel are immense and of the birds that go south in autumn a great proportion have never made the journey before. They fly the ages-old route with no knowledge (except an ancestral one) of their destination or of what lies along the way. They are the recently-hatched birds of the year, a few months old and without much skill or experience. Many never make the return trip.

We see about twenty species during the migrations—big yellowlegs and plovers that are easily recognized and bewildering swarms of the smaller kinds. These are confusing; some are larger or smaller, some have black legs, others green; some bills are long, others not quite as long and none ever stays still to permit a good look.

One of the most numerous on the beaches of the Pacific is the dunlin, or what we used to call the red-backed sandpiper. In winter the dunlin is softly coloured in greyish-brown but in spring becomes distinctively marked in rufous and black. Stockily-built, with a downward bend to its bill, it is one of the more easily identified shorebirds.

It is quite usual to see a flock in which most of the birds are in winter plumage and others partially or wholly in the more noticeable plumage of spring. Thus, in the painting of dunlins, two are winter birds with a few summer feathers beginning to show on their backs while the one on the right is completely in the breeding dress.

Dunlins move in restless, constantly shifting flocks, often with sanderlings and Aleutian sandpipers. At the height of the migrations these flocks may contain several hundred birds, and I have seen them covering the smooth sands of an Oregon beach, in higher numbers than I cared to estimate.

With dunlins or any of the little sandpipers collectively called "peeps," there is a feeling of constant, dynamic activity. A flock wheels in, alights and begins to feed running along the tideline, searching and dabbing in the cast-up wrack and debris. Suddenly, they take wing with a chorus of subdued cries. They twist away, jinking and turning in the air, flashing white and dark as the light strikes underparts and backs. They settle and rise, settle and rise again, seldom at rest.

They seem abundant now but again if we read of days a hundred years ago, we realize how sadly depleted their numbers are. In 1832, Alexander Wilson described flocks of dunlins "so great as to seem like a large cloud of thick smoke, varying in form and appearance every instant...." Great sport was to be had. The single discharge of a gun into so dense a throng would strike down a dozen or a score or, in the recorded case of one lucky fowler, ninety-six. At first the birds would bunch and hover over the fallen but later in the season they learned to be more wary. In those days you could kill and kill; though the dead lay in bushels, the numbers of the living seemed no less.

A dunlin's bill is somewhat like that of a snipe or woodcock in having a soft, slightly spatulate tip which "feels" for worms underground. With a characteristic probing action it is thrust, mandibles apart, deep into the sand or the mud of tidal estuaries. In addition to things below the surface of the ground, dunlins eat all the little animals found on beaches or in shallow water—sand flies and fleas and so on. The incoming waves may wash over their toes but the birds do not mind. When out of their depth they swim as buoyantly as ducks.

The vast majority of shorebirds nest beyond the tree line on the arctic tundra and so do dunlins. In their nuptial dress, which seems so bright yet which so perfectly matches the lichens and grass, they court and display very prettily at the beginning of the season. The males have a sweet, trilling love song which they pour forth in an ecstasy of quivering wings as they hover above the females. As well as being wooed by song, the prospective brides are pursued through the air by one or more suitors in a game which seems to be "chase and follow but don't catch." After the singing and pursuing is done and the choices have been made, the paired birds find sites to hatch and raise their families. So many enemies there are to eat the eggs and steal the chicks: ravens, foxes, jaegers and gulls all wait for an unguarded moment to strike.

The young are downy and able to run about within a short time of hatching. They forage for themselves in the company of their parents until well-grown and able to fly.

In July and August the first of the migrants, those that have nested earliest or been hatched first, start trickling south down the coast. They are the advance guards of the thousands that will soon stream along the same passage to the southern states or beyond to Argentina and Patagonia.

18 Sanderling
Calidris alba

The sanderling is a favourite of mine. Easy to recognize, bearing a dashing and descriptive name, it captures the imagination rather as, among the songbirds, the Maryland yellowthroat used to do. Sadly, that bird is called simply "yellowthroat" now, having lost the "Maryland" and with it some of the romance. But the sanderling is still its distinctive self and as attractive as ever.

To us it is a fall and sometime winter bird and a migrant of the early spring. In the plumage of these months it shows as the lightest-coloured of the small shorebirds that trill and patter semi-annually along our coastline. Compared with the cryptic buff-and-brown speckled feathering of its relatives, the sanderling is noticeably whiter—snowy below and grey, almost silvery above. To me, its plump, pale form and twinkling black legs give it a good-humoured, satisfied appearance so that when a party of sanderlings wheels into the wind and alights before me, my mood lightens.

Almost all the waders spend their winter somewhere under the Southern Cross, returning each year to nest in the far north, in what may be their ancestral home. The sanderlings go farther than almost any others; for them the chosen breeding places lie in the most northerly of the arctic islands. There they hatch their young in a shallow cup lined with a few scraps of grass. Generally, they prefer some hard, rather stony piece of ground and place the nest next to a clump of *Dryas* not far from water. The eggs are said to be buffy olive or greenish with specklings of darker. To oologists of earlier days, those connoisseurs of egg beauty, they were not particularly "showy" or attractive; nevertheless, any collector might have been glad of a clutch, for the nest of the sanderling had been seen by only a few people.

The days of late May and early June see the first hardy travellers reach the arctic where they will spend the summer. Upon their arrival they will certainly find ice still on the ponds and they may have to endure days of freezing snow and cold with little insect life to sustain them. Then they feed on buds and perhaps on whatever berries may be left over from the previous season. Though the weather may still be inclement and cold, the colour of the sanderling's plumage has become warmer. A spring moult and the wearing away of pale feather tips has changed the little "whities" to a warm reddish buff, streaked and marked in a way that will make them difficult to see on their nests.

With the thaw, courtship flights of the males begin. Ecstatically airborne, they flutter above their passively indifferent would-be mates until their wooing is successful. Egg-laying is completed by the end of June and some twenty-four days later the eggs chip and the four young emerge—determined downy puffs that as soon as dry follow their parents to the edge of the nearest water. Under the tutelage of the adults they industriously hunt insects till summer's end. In two weeks they are able to fly, though still with patches of down clinging incongruously to their new plumage.

Sanderlings are familiar to most people only on migration. They sweep north and south along both the Pacific and Atlantic coasts of America and also inland east of the Rocky Mountains. We see them usually in small parties of a dozen or so travelling by themselves, but now and then a single one will join a flock of some other kind and then its white, robust appearance makes it very conspicuous. While the other "peeps" dab and peck along the tideline, the sanderlings probe the sand deeply with partly open bills, making rows of holes as they seek out the sandfleas and tiny crustaceans that lie below the surface. Where the sandfleas hop and leap in the cast-up weed and spindrift, the sanderlings dart after them, advancing and retreating along the tide-edge in rhythm with the pulse of the waves.

As they feed almost at one's feet they seem oblivious to danger and very tame, yet I am told that large migrating flocks, resting beyond the beaches in the marshy lee formed by driftwood and dunes, are wild and very wary.

19 Glaucous-winged Gull

Larus glaucescens

Several species of gull inhabit the Pacific coast but the glaucous-winged gull is the most common and characteristic—a true native of the northwest. It is found everywhere from the Bering Sea to California and it would be difficult to visit the shore anywhere between these areas and not see this big grey-mantled gull in considerable numbers.

Many kinds of gulls have black on the wing-tips but, as can be seen in the accompanying painting, in this species the wings are all grey, the tips being merely a darker shade. In the north it is replaced by the much paler, almost white glaucous gull and in the south by the darker-mantled western gull, the present species being in a way intermediate between the two.

Gulls eat practically anything. They scavenge on the beaches, glut themselves on fish-heads and entrails at the canneries and sealing stations, follow the ferries to snatch the refuse, and beg for bread in city parks. The largest piece of food is eagerly accepted and if it is too big to be eaten at once, the bird swallows what it can and waits for that part to digest before giving another gulp. I have seen one standing with the arms of a purple star-fish protruding from its open bill and more than once have watched a gull with a large rib-bone halfway down its distorted throat and the other half protruding from its gaping mouth. Large objects like these take several hours to digest but gulls are patient.

Of course, gulls also feed on shell-fish and they have learned what the crows know—that if you fly up with a clam and drop it on the rocks or beach, sooner or later it will break, exposing the inside. It would be interesting to know which species learned the trick first.

Glaucous-winged gulls are colonial nesters and breed by themselves or with other seabirds on rocky islands up and down the coast. As the breeding season approaches, the courting pairs can be seen performing their elaborate ritual of love, bowing, walking side-by-side and turning away their heads, each gesture fixed and with definite meaning to the two involved and to outsiders. People living near a beach are awakened at first light by their strident "long calls."

Nests are built on rocky ledges, in grassy corners or under salal bushes, always out of its neighbour's reach. One observer noted that in a colony he visited, the sheltered sites were occupied by the oldest birds, the younger ones making do with more exposed places where they were liable to be robbed by crows. The nest is not much: kelp, sea- and rock-weed with a few fish bones and feathers being the material. Three eggs are usual, though a clutch of two is common.

When hatched, the young are buffy-grey with brown markings and are very hard to see against their background. They are able to run about and are fed by their parents on regurgitated food. I once helped band a lot of young gulls on an island off Victoria and found that the babies can regurgitate as well as the adults. On the second time around, the food is even less palatable and along with other things made for a very evil-smelling afternoon. When fully fledged the young birds, long since able to feed themselves, follow the adults about with hunched shoulders, begging with an upward toss of the head and whining *Mew!*

Gulls take three or four years to reach a completely mature plumage, becoming progressively lighter as time advances. The first plumage is a deep grey-brown, mottled on the wings and underparts and almost solid on the head and tail. During the next year grey appears on the back and wings while the dusky markings become paler. The head is the last to become white and even adults have mottled heads in winter. The red spot on the lower mandible of many kinds of gulls is apparently a "pecking target" for the young. When hungry they strike at this spot with their bills, an action which triggers the regurgitating response of the parent. When the spot is artificially covered, nothing happens. In the Galapagos Islands there is a gull that feeds its young at night to avoid predation and in this species the pecking spot is white!

All gulls, if they are not of the inland variety like Franklin's gull, dear to Mormon settlers, are coast-loving birds that never go more than a few miles out to sea. Shipwrecked sailors know this (if they have studied their survival books beforehand), and realize that when gulls are seen, land is near.

Glaucous-winged gulls migrate south as far as California and are found in winter even in the northern part of their range whenever there is open water.

20 Bonaparte's Gull

Larus philadelphia

This is one of those incongruous things, a gull that nests in trees. At other times of the year its habits are as marine as any other's, but in spring the Bonaparte's gull journeys overland to the shores of interior lakes. It has a wide distribution over many parts of North America and in the west it resorts at this season to the Cariboo in British Columbia and to other points north in Alaska.

Unlike its mostly ground-nesting relatives, the small, delicately-made Bonaparte's gull builds a nest anywhere from five to twenty feet up on the limb of a lakeside conifer. The shallow cup, reminiscent of a pigeon's nest, is lined with dried grass and moss and has a foundation of twigs and small sticks. In it are laid two to four buffy, typically gull-like, speckled eggs. The young hatch downy and able to move about although they stay in the nest area for some time. What a Bonaparte chick feels when it dries off and finds itself twenty feet up in a spruce, I don't know, for there is nowhere to go but down.

By mid-summer, sometime in July, flocks of these handsome gulls start to appear on the coast. They are migrants returning from the interior and at first most are dark-headed adults just beginning to lose their breeding plumage. Soon they are joined by the year's crop of young birds with black-banded tails and, on their wings, dark markings that obscure many of the feathers. These field-marks distinguish immature birds from winter adults that, like the young, wear no hoods but only black "ear-muffs" and traces of black on their heads. Even in winter plumage, the long white triangle on the fore-edge of the wings sets these gulls apart from the other species. Their flight has a characteristic buoyancy and the powered downstrokes seem especially forceful and deliberate.

Much smaller than other gulls we see in their company, Bonapartes are almost tern-like in the air. As they wheel and hover, picking small things from the water's surface, they are a pretty spectacle. From childhood days when I first came to know them, these gulls have been favourites of mine. At low tide they search the shallows and sands for little crustaceans beached by the retreating water; walking actions are as precise as their flight is graceful.

The cries of Bonaparte's gulls, in keeping with their appearance, are somewhat less coarse than those of larger gulls. The sound reminds me always of a reel as a salmon takes the lure and runs with the line. I do not know how else to describe it—a repetitive, buzzing whine, heard most frequently when the birds are foraging or resting on the shore. When disturbed at the nest, their screams are loud and prolonged.

In March there is a partial moult and the breeding plumage is assumed. Timing varies a good deal with individual birds and as late as April some birds in a flock of Bonaparte's gulls may still be improperly attired for the forthcoming season of courtship and nesting.

The lovely rosy blush that suffuses the underparts of the foreground bird in the painting is part of the breeding dress. It is very hard to see in the field and is an evanescent shade that, upon the death of the gull, quickly fades to white. This elusive pink appears on several of the "black-headed" gull species and a few others such as the American merganser. It is the subtlest and most transitory colour of all.

21 Common Murre

Uria aalge

The penguin's look-alike in the northern hemisphere is the murre. A trim seabird that also wears black and white "evening dress," it stands in an upright, penguin-like posture on the rocks of its breeding colonies, looking superficially much like its counterparts in the southern hemisphere. Of course, the relationship is distant and the similarities slight. Murres are not flightless as penguins are, and parallels in outward appearance are simply the result of species solving common problems in the same way.

From the coast of California north to the Pribiloffs murres of the Pacific breed in noisy, crowded colonies that cover the rocky ledges and fill the sea caves of offshore islands with birds, eggs, chicks and guano. The sites are shared with gulls, cormorants and other seabirds, each pair with a few feet or inches of territory which it vigorously defends. The female murre lays a single egg, shaped to roll in a tight circle and thus remain on its narrow, nestless shelf. It is guarded vigilantly by the parents and only their watchfulness protects egg or baby from the screaming, wheeling, predatory and ever-present gulls. Sharp-eyed and protective though they are, the murres lose many eggs and young offspring to the gulls that sidle about awaiting an opportunity to snatch and steal.

At the time of hatching, the young murre is covered in woolly down, dark brownish above and white below. At first it rests quietly on its tarsi, waiting for feeding time; the parents give it semi-digested food and later, when it is older and more active, small fish of various kinds.

The murres leave the seabird colonies much earlier than do other species with which they share the rocks. Their chicks are only a few weeks old and still unable to fly when the adults begin to call from below the ledges, urging the young birds to enter the water. In their anxiety to obey, the chicks scramble and tumble down the cliffs, peeping excitedly in reply. Once in the water, they are escorted by their parents to the open sea where all remain until spring.

At the end of the summer the young murres have white throats and faces and resemble the adults, which at this time assume their winter plumage. In fall many can be seen in some stage intermediate between the two plumages and there is scarcely time for the completion of one moult before a second in early winter puts them again in the handsome, sharply-defined plumage of the breeding season.

They seldom come near shore in winter and any murre seen close in at that time is likely to be ill or touched by oil. Needless to say, they suffer badly when oil spills occur on their fishing grounds. A small spot on the plumage is sufficient to kill a seabird, for oil mats the feathers and destroys the insulation between the bird's skin and the frigid water. There is hardly a sight more pitiful than a sodden, doomed murre pathetically trying to clean its fouled plumage.

In early April the murres arrive on their breeding grounds, descending on the islands in numbers and then capriciously abandoning them again for a day or two. As the nesting urge becomes imperative they come to stay, establish their small territories, and lay their eggs. Most have courted and chosen their mates during migration but as the colony organizes there is still much ritual bowing and posturing. Each time a murre lands on its ledge it must run a gauntlet of jabbing bills as it pushes past other families to reach its own nest. As there is always much coming and going in the colony, this lends an air of restless disquiet to the scene.

Though their wings are narrow and small in proportion to their bodies, murres are strong fliers. On migration they may fly high in little groups, though the usual flight is rapid and low over the surface of the sea. They live largely on fish and are excellent divers, using their wings to propel them swiftly underwater in pursuit of their agile and elusive prey.

Happily for the murres, "egging" is a thing of the past but in days gone by millions of eggs were taken by bands of commercial egg collectors who camped on the islands in the breeding season and decimated the colonies to such an extent that the species was seriously threatened with extermination. Now that the practice is prohibited and the market dead, murres are left alone and have recovered something close to their former numbers.

22 Pigeon Guillemot

Cepphus columba

Compact and neckless, looking like painted wooden toys, they paddle placidly among the myriad islands of the Pacific northwest. With an upending flip and a flash of scarlet feet they disappear below the surface, to bob up cork-like a few moments later. These are pigeon guillemots, unobtrusive little relatives of the murres and auklets, cousins to the bizarre puffin.

In summer they may be recognized by an all-black plumage and large white wing patches, but with the fall moult their appearance alters completely and for the next few months they resemble the bird in the painting. Then, I suppose, they might be confused with murres, though they are smaller. The two species look not unalike in winter but the guillemot's wing patches still show and when it flies or dives, the red feet banish any doubt.

Along the whole Pacific coast this is a common and widely distributed species though not really abundant in the sense that large flocks are seen. Generally, one or two are in sight at a time.

Guillemots nest in the seabird colonies with other species and choose a variety of sites. They may use burrows which they excavate themselves high on the cliffs, or may simply nest on the shingle in the lee of a large boulder. Many California nests are on rock shelves and ledges deep within the recesses of sea caves. Always they seek to raise their families in sheltered places that are away from the light and protected from view.

As the guillemots begin to gather near their breeding places there are some spirited encounters to be witnessed between rival males. They face each other with raised tails and open, scarlet mouths in quarrels that are very often bluff. However, frequently they engage each other in violent scuffles that begin on the surface of the sea and continue below. The loser breaks away first.

Two eggs are laid in mid-May or even later in high latitudes. They nest on the ground in a slight hollow with a few chips of stone, but it is uncertain whether the guillemots bring them, or simply choose places where the chips have collected.

The incubation period is twenty-one days and the young enter the world clothed in down of a sooty shade that pales somewhat as they grow. They are not beautiful; their graceless bodies squat on the oversized tarsi as, pressed into the dark corners of their refuge, they wait to be fed. The parents bring them small fishes for every meal. Though fat, the young are nimble and quick to scuttle away at the threat of danger, for they have many enemies waiting outside. They do not leave the nest until fully-fledged and ready to take to the sea.

In warm weather, the adult "sea pigeons" can be seen sunning themselves on the rocks, trim little figures standing upright on bright red feet. They take all their food—mostly fish—underwater and in pursuit they rely on their wings, unlike loons and grebes which use only their feet, except when hard-pressed.

The flight of the guillemot is strong, though their small, narrow wings seem inadequate to sustain the heavy bodies in the air. Perhaps they are not very supple but they are quite fast. When put up by a boat, they buzz away on blurred wings in a long curve, to plop down again astern.

23 Marbled Murrelet

Brachyramphus marmoratus

At the turn of the century there were still some mysteries in North American ornithology. The breeding grounds and nests of more than one bird remained unknown and puzzled eminent naturalists of the day. One such undiscovered nest was that of the marbled murrelet. Few question marks still stand: Ross' goose, the black swift and the bristle-thighed curlew all have yielded their long-kept secrets. So, finally, has the marbled murrelet, though only very recently. Its breeding habits, the whereabouts and description of its nest remained for years unknown, the last riddle of its kind to engage us.

A commonly seen little seabird of the north Pacific, the marbled murrelet lives in littoral waters—the inside passages, straits and sounds between outlying islands and the mainland. Most members of its family, the other murrelets, the auklets, murres and puffins, stay farther out but this species is found close to land. At any time it can be seen up and down the coast, floating woodenly on the water or working the tide-rips with quick, flip-up dives for the little fish and crustaceans that form its dietary staple.

On twilit summer evenings its cries are heard across the water of the bays and inlets. At this time of day the murrelets become restless as they prepare to relieve their incubating mates or to carry fish to feed the downy young. They rise from the water's surface as the light fails, circling higher and higher on little whirring wings and heading toward the distant timbered slopes. Each bird flies for miles and in almost complete darkness must home in to its own mate and few square inches of nest. As the birds ascend in the deepening night, a last glimmer is struck from the silver fish in their bills; then only the voices tell of their presence in the air above.

In the morning, the murrelets are back. Where have they been? Where do they nest? There have been several theories: that they nested in island burrows; on inaccessible cliff-faces; in or among trees deep within the forest; or possibly, like Kittlitz's murrelet, above the mountain snow-line.

Many people tried to find the solution. In 1930, S.J. Darcus, an oologist, believed he had found proof of the murrelets' nesting in burrows on the Queen Charlotte Islands. His claim was not backed by specimens and, sadly for him, he was not believed. One or two other unsubstantiated claims were also made. The burrow idea was one of the first to go. Charles Guiguet, an ornithologist who has spent nearly forty years studying the birds and mammals of the Pacific northwest, examined every likely island and potential breeding place. He never found the slightest evidence to support the theory and, by the lack of the typical "burrow odour" on chicks, judged that they did not come from below ground.

Nor was anything found to suggest cliffs as the site, yet to some field-workers this seemed the likeliest possibility. However, murrelets are seen flying over and sometimes into the timber, while at night their voices are heard passing high over hills and mountains at great distances from the sea. Once or twice a felled tree has yielded a shattered egg. I remember one—the yellow-green fragments darkly blotched—that came to the B.C. Provincial Museum when I worked there in high school summers. These finds, together with the picking up of occasional young birds with down still adhering to their heads, in the forest, on roads and once on the campus of the University of British Columbia, strongly indicated a tree-nesting habit. Quite recently, there came a Russian discovery in the small trees of the taiga. Also, in California a nest has been found on the thick limb of a Douglas fir, a hundred and forty feet above ground. A downy young and egg fragments were shaken out and recovered, proving tree-nesting a fact.

The arrival of the young on the water is dramatic, and quite in keeping with the element of mystery in their life history. Late in the season, murrelets may be seen congregating in unusual numbers before their evening departure. After much agitated calling they take their leave, and upon their dawn return are accompanied, each pair, by a single fully-fledged, grey and white chick, similar in appearance to the winter adult shown in the painting.

The marbled murrelet kept its secret well, and no wonder. It is less than a foot in length and in spring is obscurely dressed in sooty umber brown. Only by night does it leave and return to its nest, and when the chick is well grown the parent is absent except for the single nocturnal feeding. Who, in the impenetrable night of a west coast forest, could witness the arrival, brief exchange and departure of this little creature, more than a hundred feet above in the dense fir canopy? . . . No-one.

24 Tufted Puffin

Lunda cirrhata

In spring the precipitous cliffs and slopes of the north coast's islands are decorated with nesting seabirds. The ledges are lined with murres, whose black and white is punctuated at intervals by dark, reptilian cormorants that stare from evil-smelling structures on the white-splashed rocks. On clutches of eggs hidden in patches of sea-pink or under low-growing bushes, gulls settle in snowy devotion.

No bird here presents an appearance as startlingly bizarre as that of the tufted puffins. Hundreds can be seen standing close by the mouths of their nesting burrows in the rank growth of the island sides; compact black bodies erect, they remain alert and sentinel-like on stout orange legs. Red-rimmed eyes gaze from quaint white masks that, along with large bright bills and wind-blown plumes of straw, give them a curious air.

On the Queen Charlotte and Aleutian Islands tufted puffins are among the most numerous breeding seabirds. In places their burrows perforate the ground so closely that one must place one's foot carefully to avoid breaking through the tunnels. These are sometimes shallow enough for the end to be seen but usually are somewhat deeper. In the chamber at the far end a single egg is laid, and incubation is shared by the parents. Each does about a twelve-hour spell of duty with the changeover occurring as darkness falls.

Anyone imprudent enough to thrust an unprotected hand down an occupied burrow will receive a savage bite, for puffins' bills are sharp and their jaws powerful enough to shear off or crush shell-fish.

Near the breeding islands lines of these strange-looking but beautiful birds may be seen passing to and from their fishing grounds, often at some distance from the colonies. Like other members of their family, puffins have small and narrow wings in proportion to the size and weight of their bodies. Consequently, though their flight is swift and direct, they have little manoeuvrability in the air and are unable to turn sharply or climb steeply. Getting airborne from the water's surface is laborious but from their breeding heights it is simpler—the birds drop from the sheer cliffs, free-falling until they gain sufficient momentum.

Tufted puffins have always been a source of food, clothing and ornaments for island natives. These people, taking advantage of the birds' flying style, catch them deftly by suddenly thrusting long-handled nets in their flight paths.

The tufted puffins' own food, of course, lies in the products of the sea and consists largely of fish such as sand lance and herring that are caught in swift underwater pursuit. Crustacea and molluscs make up a proportion of the diet in addition to fish. These birds are so good at diving and capturing their chosen prey that they bear the enmity of many fishermen whose vessels they follow.

Photographs are sometimes seen showing puffins carrying neat rows of fishes, head to tail, in their bills. These birds are parents of burrow-bound fledglings and are returning to the colonies with food for their young. Coming in on rapidly beating wings they are an amusing and attractive sight, each one bearing its shining burden.

In winter much of the puffins' nuptial finery is lost. The bill becomes smaller through the shedding of part of its horny ornamentation and the long filamentous plumes are moulted. In winter, the white face of the adults and young of the year, giving in spring such a clown-like appearance, is replaced by dark feathers. Altogether, puffins in the off-season and those that have not attained maturity scarcely resemble their boldly-painted spring selves.

25 Band-tailed Pigeon
Columba fasciata

A large holly tree grows by a window of my home in Victoria and I once saw it beautifully decorated: on a pale February day a flock of hungry band-tailed pigeons descended to feed on the berries and for more than an hour the viewers indoors had a chance to admire at close range the subtle shades of plumage. Over the whole tree pigeons teetered and stretched with fluttering wings and spread tails as they sought to reach clusters on the outermost twigs. How lovely they were; they filled their crops with bright fruit, while we behind the window-pane feasted in another way.

This fine "wild pigeon" has been a popular game bird since the early days of western settlement and, unless it has been feeding on cascara berries, is very good to eat. In the bad days of the market hunters, fifty to a hundred years ago, the band-tail was reduced to almost nothing. Many species shared that experience and travelled by the wagon-load to the edge of extinction. Some, such as the passenger pigeon and the great auk, did not return at all, but became legendary names of nostalgia and bitter regret. After one particularly destructive blood-bath in the winter of 1911 when eager sportsmen destroyed an estimated half of the band-tail population, the species was afforded protection in the form of a five-year shooting ban and, later, regulated killing.

They have made a fine recovery and once more the scattered flocks are a familiar sight as they pass, high and arrow-swift, over the fir-clad hillsides.

The deep, insistent cooing of the pigeons is heard in spring, when the males indulge in a strange kind of courtship flight, no doubt to engage the affections of their prospective mates. I have watched it many times over my garden: with fanned tail and stiffly-held wings that seem to beat only at the tips, a bird will make a slow circling flight of perhaps forty or fifty feet, returning to the point of departure. The performance is accompanied by a curious churring, wheezing call that others as well as I have found difficult to describe. At one time it was thought to be produced by the wings but to me always seemed vocal, as it has since proven to be.

Band-tails build the usual type of pigeon nest, a saucer-shaped structure of coarse twigs, hardly more than a platform and very loosely put together; so loosely, in fact, that removing the nest usually results in its falling apart.

In widely scattered communities (they could not be called colonies), the pigeons raise one squab apiece, feeding it that unique substance "pigeon's milk" a whitish fluid secreted in the throat lining of the adults.

This species feeds mostly on various nuts and a wide assortment of berries and other fruits. On southern Vancouver Island they will venture onto backyard lawns for the acorns of the Garry oak and where oaks are plentiful, the acorns form a major item of diet. Waste grain is gleaned from fields and farmyards; a few even come to feed now and then with the domestic pigeons at my studio, but shyly and only when I am not in sight.

The seasonal nature of most of their food necessitates a lot of moving about from place to place as local supplies are exhausted. An abundant crop of some favourite item will attract the pigeons in large numbers and they will stay until it is gone, afterwards moving on in their opportunist wandering which is their nearest approach to real migration.

26 Snowy Owl

Nyctaea scandiaca

Snowy owls, ghostly predators of the polar regions, leave their native tundra at intervals to invade latitudes far to the south. As more or less regular migrations, the invasions occur in winter and are directly connected with shortages of the owls' staple arctic food, lemmings.

When lemmings are plentiful, the owls and foxes live high and produce many fat young. When there is a serious decline in rodent numbers the snowy owls leave. On silent wings they drift out of the north like huge snowflakes to settle on the rocks and fenceposts of a more southerly land far less harsh and uncompromising than their own. They come to us quite regularly every four or five years, sometimes appearing in quantity across the whole continent.

Because of their conspicuous size and white colour they attract a good deal of human attention, much of it not to their advantage. In earlier times, sad to say, few owls that journeyed south lived to see their homeland again. They fell to the gun of every sportsman in the country and taxidermists were kept busy mounting white owls by the hundreds for cigar store windows and farmhouse parlours. I like to believe they fare better these days and that many return to the tundra in the spring.

In the winter of 1973-74 numbers of snowy owls descended upon the west coast and probably on other parts of the country as well. They stayed from November until March and I received many reports of white owls perched atop houses and television masts and even on cars. They became so commonplace that it was hardly a surprise to see a great pale form sitting motionless on the rocky shore or peering cat-eyed from a low, bare tree.

In the arctic they live principally on lemmings and ptarmigan, and in summer on the many species of birds that go north to breed. However, they are not choosy eaters and on occasion they will take any prey, from big arctic hares to little buntings and longspurs. Snowy owls wintering on the coast must take a heavy toll of the ducks and seabirds that are so plentiful. A large, darkly-barred female spent several months on a golf course half a mile from my home; from her favourite vantage point she had only to look down the fairway to take her pick from the grazing flocks of wigeon. Nearby in the kelp beds were harlequins and scaups while on the wave-wet rocks beside her clambered the little turnstones and surfbirds. Easy living.

In spite of their imposing appearance these birds are not above a bit of scavenging. Last winter I was told of ten that had gathered about the carcass of a beached whale. They were feeding upon it, a tasty and endless source of meat that needed no catching. There is something ignominious in the sight of a bird such as a snowy owl, so eminently able to capture and kill, picking at carrion. But even superb hunters take the easy way occasionally.

As might be expected of raptors which live near water and have catholic tastes, snowy owls are skilled fishers. They use the eagle's style of swoop-and-snatch as well as their own method of waiting crouched by a poolside to grab a fish with a single swipe of a feathered foot.

Nesting on the ground—in the high arctic there is little choice—snowy owls raise four to ten grey-downed, hungry young. At this season, the brief bright summer, other tundra nesters suffer depredation, for the nursery diet of owlets consists of ptarmigan chicks and small birds as well as of rodents. The nests are always built on knolls or hillocks, the highest, driest places to be found. In fact, elevations of this sort are prerequisites for good owl country and are used not only for nesting but as lookout points and places for courting birds to display. In good times, snowy owls dot the landscape like snowmen, each on its own rise.

The young owls do not all hatch at the same time and there is as much as two days between the time the first chick breaks its shell and the appearance of the next. Consequently, the first few of a brood are usually well-grown and fledged by the time the last come forth into the world.

Incubation is undertaken by the female while her smaller, much whiter and less maculate mate brings her food and protects the nest. The adults are too large and formidable to fear anything very much except man but the chicks need careful guarding. Arctic foxes and jaegers, sharp-eyed and unflagging thieves of the barrens, are quick to destroy a nest in a parent's moment of carelessness.

Snowy owls utter deep hooting and booming notes during their courtship. The males in display are said by Dr. Sutton to puff out their throat feathers enormously and to elevate their tails as they call. In this exaggerated posture they strut stiff-legged on their hillocks, in an ecstasy of spring feeling. At other times, like other owls they can whistle, rattle and make a lot of strange sounds that probably don't help to make the long arctic night less eerie and desolate.

27 Pygmy Owl
Glaucidium gnoma

The most immediately striking thing about a pygmy owl is its diminutive size; in bulk much less than a robin, it is scarcely larger than some of the songbirds it takes. Only that miniscule desert-dweller, the elf owl, is smaller.

Though little, the pygmy is a formidable bird of prey that never hesitates to attack creatures twice its size and weight. The courage and determination that lead it to tackle prey much larger than itself have given it a rather gory reputation. "Bloodthirsty" and "savage" are epithets sometimes applied to it, yet, in reality, it is no wanton killer. When a pygmy owl is hungry it hunts; when satisfied it rests in the evergreens or sits with feathers puffed out in the sun. Mice, insects, frogs and lizards form a large part of its food though many small birds are eaten, too. The menu varies from place to place and according to the availability and abundance of one or another item.

Metaphorically speaking, pygmy owls sometimes bite off more than they can chew. They have been seen struggling with ground squirrels in what would seem very unequal contests. Though the owls are often victorious, one was found with its claws locked into a mole and apparently unable either to fly with its weighty burden or to extricate itself.

A pygmy owl, the least of the northwest's avian predators, is feared and detested by all small birds. They all recognize the pygmy as a potential threat and almost always react violently to the sight or sound of one. Those most in danger, such as kinglets or juncos, show the greatest consternation but, though they mob the owl, they keep a discreet distance. On the other hand, Steller's jays and whiskey jacks are fearless and in some instances have been known to kill the pygmies, in a reversal of the usual order.

This species is active in the daylight and it may be heard calling at any hour. It has a number of fairly melodious sounds in its vocabulary. One is a single syllable note repeated two or three times; it may be imitated quite easily by half-whistling, half-speaking the drawn-out word *hook* or *cook*. The author is difficult to locate and may be much farther away than suspected for the sound carries far and is deceptively ventriloqual. At close range the note is heard to be more complex with a sibilant beginning and a sort of gurgling finish. Another call, the song of the pygmy owl, resembles the quaver of a screech owl but is lighter in quality and not as mellow. Even this little trill is followed by the characteristically spaced *hook—hook*.

To a chickadee or a vireo a pygmy owl located is better than one unseen. Thus, the mobbing of this and of other raptors may give some fleeting measure of safety to the small birds. As long as they keep the object of their fear in view they have a good chance of avoiding its grasp. However, their attention span is short, and after a little time the owl is left in peace. Ornithologists and collectors, knowing the songbird's propensity to bully owls, have long used the pygmy owl's call to bring hard-to-obtain species within range of their guns.

The *hook—hook* has been described as the master call of the woods and whether real or counterfeit quickly draws the attention of every bird in the neighbourhood, including any pygmy owl that happens to be near. P.A. Taverner, author of the old *Birds of Canada* that I so loved as a child, wrote that once he shot an olive-sided flycatcher only to have it snatched up by a pygmy owl that he had inadvertantly lured.

Like many of the smaller owls, this one nests in holes. As it does not excavate on its own, nesting sites are the abandoned homes of other birds. These holes, generally made by flickers or hairy woodpeckers, are seldom more than twenty feet above ground and often much lower. On the floor of the cavity with a few chips and feathers to cushion them, four eggs are laid, to be hatched early in July. The young birds are tended mostly by the mother and they stay in the nest for about four weeks before venturing forth.

The pygmy owl inhabits the high slopes of the mountains and in various races is found from Alaska to Guatemala. In Canada it occurs in the Rocky Mountains and the coast ranges and in the United States may be found as far east as Colorado.

Pygmies like the forests of fir and pine at the higher elevations and prefer never to be far from the edge of the timber. Very cold weather may bring them down nearer sea level, but not for long as they are mountain birds and able to withstand quite severe conditions. A good place to look for them is on one of the scarred and logged-off hillsides that the lumber companies leave in a tangle of stumps and slash. Here, with few standing trees to impede the view, a little imitative whistling may bring a pygmy flitting from one skeleton snag to another, all indignation and pugnacity, to seek the supposed interloper.

These owls are commoner than generally supposed; quite often they are not recognized. Their flight is direct, resembling that of the shrike, with none of the mothy quality expected of owls. Then, too, their size is misleading, for we do not think of birds of prey as being so small.

J.F. LANSDOWNE
-1973-

28 Short-eared Owl

Asio flammeus

In his beautiful book *The Peregrine*, J.A. Baker used his gift for imagery when speaking of short-eared owls "breathing out of the grass." So they appear to do, for these silent creatures seem almost weightless as they rock and sway in the updraughts of the flat land.

They are most active in the half-light of dusk and dawn yet they hunt during the day and because of this we see them oftener than other owls. Warmly pale and buoyant, they quarter the fields and marshes methodically, beating back and forth low over the ground. Every little while one will check, hover for a few seconds and either pass on or drop down with raised wings and extended feet.

The usual food of short-eared owls is mammals such as mice and voles which generally make up the greater part, as well as numerous insects and a few small birds. These last range from sparrows and meadowlarks up to larger birds the size of flickers.

It has been noted many times that when mice or other rodents become unusually abundant and reach plague proportions, short-eared owls appear in great numbers to feed upon them. Dozens of owls descend on a few square miles of infested land and, in feasting, do an incalculable service to farmers. A single owl hunting just to sustain itself will take a surprising number of mice and when there are young to be fed that number increases tremendously. Anywhere from four to nine chicks are raised and it has been learned that two half-grown owlets require twelve to fifteen house sparrows or the equivalent each day to satisfy their hunger.

The courtship of these birds is intriguing and beautiful to watch. The male sails and glides in the air, spiralling higher and higher with slow, deliberate wing-beats. He swoops in shallow dives and towers effortlessly again. As he dives a fluttering sound is heard, like the beating of a small bird against the bars of a cage. The origin of the sound was a mystery until it was seen that the bird held its wings below its body and struck the tips together sharply and rapidly.

Short-eared owls live where trees are few and the most elevated points are bushes or fence posts. They can be seen quite often resting on these but for the most part they sit on the ground. It is very difficult to tell whether the object before you is a lichen-covered stump or a clod or a motionless owl. Many a clearly inanimate part of the scenery has suddenly spread wings and drifted away. The owl's colouring blends perfectly with the earth and at first glance the weird countenance resembles no bird's. Only the charcoal-rimmed eyes glow hotly from the savage, unearthly face.

Nests are placed on the ground. At best they are shallow depressions sparingly lined with grass and a few feathers. The feathers may be simply dinnertime leftovers but usually some attempt is made at a grass lining. Sometimes the shelter of a tussock or a rise in the ground is utilized and, exceptionally, a nest may be in a bush or even in a burrow.

The variable number of eggs laid is uncommon among birds; they can be relied upon generally to deviate very little in this way. Short-eared owls lay between four and nine eggs, with five or six being a usual number. This variability may be connected with the cyclic abundance of their normal prey: when mice are numerous there is food for a maximum number of chicks while in lean times a small family can more easily avoid starvation. How the body of the adult interprets factors such as few or many mice is unknown.

The owlets do not all hatch at once. A family of short-ears will be composed of chicks ranging in age from a few days to a week or two. When about a fortnight old they begin to stray from the nest, though still unable to fly. As they grow older they go farther and farther from the immediate environs—as much as a hundred yards. At this stage, if they are discovered by a potential enemy they may play dead and allow themselves, limp and in disarray, to be handled. More often, when escape is impossible, they turn on their backs with talons out, ready to rip. The parents show every sign of agitation and alarm when the young are threatened, diving at the intruder and decoying him away with feigned injury and impossible-to-ignore squeals and whistles.

The cries of the distressed adults are only one kind of call. There is the love song of the male, delivered in the air during courtship, as well as a two-syllable bark like a little dog's and various snoring and hissing noises. A most extraordinary cry is one I heard from a captive injured owl in Seattle. The bird was housed near my bedroom and several times in the night I heard the sound—an intense, three-second hiss that reached a sharp crescendo and then died abruptly. It was a little like a child's imitation of cars passing on a freeway and was unlike anything I had heard before from a bird.

Short-eared owls have world-wide distribution, and are found on every continent with the exception of Australia.

29 Saw-whet Owl

Aegolius acadicus

The saw-whet is one of the smallest and loveliest owls—moth-soft and delicate, with a large head and a wide-eyed look of total innocence. It is almost entirely nocturnal in its habits so that, though it may be quite plentiful in any given district, it is seldom seen by human beings.

So small itself, the saw-whet subsists to a great extent on small prey, its food consisting mainly of mice, shrews and little rodents such as young squirrels and chipmunks, and an occasional bird. Its days are spent resting in the dark recesses of the coniferous woods; pressed close to the trunk of a tree, the owl is both camouflaged and sheltered by the tangled canopy of branches. At the approach of darkness the saw-whet drops from its perch and with utterly silent flight begins hunting for the creatures that, with barely perceptible sounds, scurry across the forest floor.

This species seems not to share the pygmy owl's ferocious disposition or that bird's predeliction for attempting to capture oversized prey. But now and then a renegade saw-whet gains entrance to a pigeon loft or chicken coop and does much damage. Faced with unlimited choice and opportunity it kills and kills, eating only a small part of each hapless victim.

Glimpsed among the trees in the half-light of evening, more than one saw-whet owl has been mistaken for a woodcock, with its round-winged flight and similar size. I cannot say from experience for I have not been lucky enough to see saw-whets in the wild, but only those that in some way have become captive. I well remember as a child seeing my first saw-whet, in an office of the old Provincial Museum in Victoria. With not a breath of sound it flew to a curtain rod over the window and from there uttered a short owl-quaver so melodious and disembodied that I could not believe it came from the bird.

The accompanying picture of the saw-whet, clutching a house sparrow and looking possessive, was painted from a bird picked up on the road along the Victoria waterfront. It had been struck and killed by a car, as owls quite often are, while swooping low over the roadway.

Through parts of the country saw-whet owls sometimes migrate in quite large numbers but it is only when one comes to grief that we become aware of their presence around us. Occasionally, disaster befalls them on a larger scale. Extreme cold and snow or a freezing rain may prevent their getting food, and then dead and starving owls in pitiable condition are picked up around farms and in the woods. Also, they have been washed up in numbers on the shore after bad storms that have coincided with migration-time lake crossings.

An old woodpecker hole is considered a fine home by a saw-whet owl. The families are almost always raised in these abandoned excavations in dead tree stubs. This owl is not much of a nest-builder and the eggs are laid directly upon the floor of the cavity; anything resembling a lining is purely coincidental. In these austere surroundings the five to seven eggs are incubated and hatched. The chicks grow slowly from very small blind things into beautiful owlets clad in rich shades of cinnamon red and deep brown. This plumage is distinctly unlike that of any other young owl and its beauty is accentuated by a broad white v-shaped marking above and between the eyes.

The curious name of this bird deserves mention. People familiar with birds will know that it derives from a call uttered by the owl in spring—a loud, two-syllable note closely resembling the sound made by filing or "whetting" a saw. Neither this song nor the ringing, metallic note sometimes given is what we think of as owl-like. However, as I have mentioned, the saw-whet is capable of producing a tremulous song rather like that of a pygmy owl.

Saw-whet owls have a wide distribution. Throughout the forested regions of the west coast as well as wide areas of the rest of the continent they are not uncommon but their elusiveness and nocturnal habits make the sighting of one a rare pleasure.

J.F. LANSDOWNE
·1972·

30 Black Swift

Cypseloides niger

Swifts are among the most interesting and remarkable birds. Mysterious in their habits, puzzling and slightly sinister in their independence of the earth below them, they are familiar to most people only as dark, sickle-winged shapes circling high overhead.

The many species—most of them living in tropical latitudes—are much alike in looks and behaviour and no other group of birds is so completely adapted to aerial existence. Their particular and extreme form of specialization has made the swifts just what their name implies: very high-speed and sophisticated little flying machines.

On America's west coast, we can see two species, the cigar-bodied little Vaux's swift and the big, square-tailed black swift of the accompanying painting. Black swifts have a wide range from Alaska to Mexico and in September they appear along the coast on their southward migration. At this time one may look up and see fifty or more sailing slowly down the sky, individual birds feeding as they go but staying in a loosely grouped flock. These are birds that have bred in the northern part of their range, perhaps in Alaska or the British Columbia interior.

Black swifts, like others of their family, feed, drink, bathe and gather nesting material while on the wing. They mate and probably at times also sleep in the same insubstantial element. This last has been found to be true of the common species of Europe, so it is likely that other kinds are able to do so too.

Swifts, in a way, are often heralds of bad weather for they make temporary journeys from their base to avoid storms which cause a reduction in the quantity of flying insects. It has been found that European swifts escape poor weather more quickly by flying out of it than by waiting for it to pass. They may travel several hundred miles, flying into the wind and out of a low pressure zone, eventually passing around it and back. Black swifts seem to do this and in A.C. Bent's *Life Histories*, a contributor writes that he came to look for the birds in conjunction with foul weather in spring. Again and again they are mentioned as appearing with or just prior to the arrival of rain and wind.

For some forty-five years after the black swift came to the attention of scientists, its nest and eggs were a subject of speculation, although it was assumed to breed in mountainous places. No nest was found until a gentleman collecting cormorant eggs descended a California sea cliff and put a swift off her mud cup nest. It contained one large egg leading skeptical ornithologists to think he had come across the nest of a small petrel. We now know that in addition to sea cliffs, these swifts choose other inaccessible places as nurseries—for instance, the ever-wet rock face behind a waterfall or perhaps a cramped niche a few inches deep on the perpetually shadowed side of a narrow canyon—anywhere, in fact, that furnishes a ledge away from direct sunlight and with a sheer drop below for easy take-off and safety.

The solitary nestling cannot undertake journeys to leave the rain behind but it has a safeguard against inclement conditions; in cold rainy weather when food is scarce it is able to survive for several days without sustenance. To further conserve energy, its growth rate slows and its body temperature drops.

The adults, too, can endure short spells of cold by lapsing into a state of torpidity and may be found sometimes in this condition, clinging in crevices or chimneys. I do not think any evidence has been found to indicate that swifts truly hibernate, although at least one other bird, the poorwill, does. Perhaps the finding of torpid swifts lent strength to the belief held in Europe until the eighteenth century that swallows and swifts hibernated in winter by clumping together and settling into the muddy bottoms of ponds. To people of that time it probably seemed a more believable solution to their annual disappearance than the truth of migration.

31 Rufous Humming-bird

Selasphorus rufus

The rufous hummingbird is the only member of a largely tropical family to venture as far north as Alaska and the Yukon. Travelling each spring from its winter haunts in the mountains of Mexico it reaches the Pacific northwest in late March just as the red flower panicles of the wild currant are in full bloom. This flower is a great favourite and usually the first awareness of the hummingbird's arrival is a flash of chestnut and a throb of wings near a currant bush. Not even the first swallow is a surer or more welcome sign of winter's end.

It is the males we see first; with their burning rufous backs and throats like hot coals, they precede the females on the northward migration and arrive on their breeding grounds a week or two earlier. When the prospective mates appear the courting begins, with the males towering and diving in spectacular aerial exhibitions. Shooting almost straight up to a height of twenty or thirty feet and diving sharply down again, the quivering suitor pulls up and hovers a few inches away from the female. With expanded tail he turns left and right to display his brilliant throat patch or gorget. At the bottom of each dive he utters an invariable *dit-di-dit-dee*, which often attracts human attention to the pair that would otherwise go unnoticed.

As soon as the hummingbirds have mated and nest-building is well underway, the fiery-tempered, fiery-feathered males leave their mates and return south, neither seeing nor taking part in the raising of their young. The nest may be almost anywhere—sometimes only waist-high from the ground, sometimes twenty feet up on the swaying tip of a cedar branch.

A hummingbird once built on a cherry bough outside our kitchen window. I was no more than five, but the birds of those days stand out clearly in my mind. It was the time that they took possession of me, stamping themselves onto my mind as sharply as little *Archaeopteryx* is pressed into its bed of stone. Of other things, I really only remember the orange lino on the kitchen floor and that in winter everything froze, even the goldfish bowl and a kinglet in the woodshed. But I remember that hummingbird's nest. Simply by looking through the window we could examine the beautiful, branch-saddling structure of plant down and grey-green lichens, lashed and anchored with spider webs. In the bottom lay the two white eggs, large for the size of the bird yet still so small.

One day the eggs were gone and in their place were two lumpy black things about the size of bees or fat spiders. These just-hatched young were quite blind and featherless and their appearance was a shock. I don't know what we expected but it was not these little grotesques. Clearly no miracle could ever transform them into the vibrant hummers of our experience. However, their feathers grew and their eyes opened. Soon they were sitting side by side, filling the nest-cup, clad in iridescent green and white.

Nestlings are fed by the parent on a regurgitated fluid of insects and nectar. Thrusting her bill deep into the baby's throat the mother pumps the food down; the process is alarming to watch for it looks like an advanced and perilous form of sword-swallowing. After about twenty days of this sort of food delivery the fully-fledged young are ready to leave. They buzz away, without any preliminary practice, to spend a few weeks darting and squeaking among the late summer flowers. When fall comes they make their first long, uncharted journey south.

The incredible throat feathers of male hummingbirds fascinate everyone who has seen them. Their astonishing brilliance is derived from a faceted structure that refracts the light. The gorget of a rufous hummer is especially beautiful for it gives off rays of crimson, scarlet, yellow and even green as the bird turns.

It would not seem that anything could catch such minute, swift birds but hummingbirds do fall victim occasionally to various predators. There is an account of one that was snapped up by a fish, and hawks take them now and then for what can be hardly more than a snack. Unfortunately, cats waiting beneath bushes find them irresistible and quite easy to catch. Hummingbirds come to grief in other ways, too. Many times the little jewel-like bodies, killed against a window-pane, have been brought to me to paint. Once two males in their furious pursuit of one another dashed against some glass and were given to me in a box, stunned and trembling. For a time they aroused and buzzed around the room like squibs but they did not survive.

32 Common Flicker

Colaptes auratus

Until recently there were believed to be three species of flicker: the yellow-shafted in the east, the red-shafted in the west and in the southwestern states, the gilded flicker. But a great many birds seem to be mixtures that show endless intergradations of colour and patterns. These occur not only where the breeding populations overlap but even at the extreme outside limits of their ranges.

For example, many yellow-shafted flickers show pink on the underwings or have red feathers in their black "moustache" stripes. Red-shafted birds, on the other hand, may be tinged with yellow under the wings and some even are asymmetrical, having one black side to the moustache and one red. Their napes frequently show a red v, a mark properly belonging to eastern birds. It is now thought that perhaps a single species of flicker became separated into these races during a period of glaciation. Now that the ice has gone they are again merging.

Here is a woodpecker that has branched out into somewhat less specialized fields of endeavour. The normal woodpecker habits have not been given up entirely but flickers behave more like other birds, perching cross-ways on branches and spending much of their time on the ground instead of propped against tree trunks.

In fact, a lot of their food is taken on the ground and everyone has seen these brown-backed birds systematically probing a patch of soft earth. Much of the time they are seeking ants, for these bitter little insects are a favourite food and constitute a major portion of diet. Flickers tug out earthworms in the manner of robins and also help rid the earth of a wide assortment of grubs and other things that man dislikes. In winter when the ants and their relatives are not so much in evidence the flickers rely more heavily on plant food. Windfall apples, softened and fermented by the frost, are appreciated then and in season all manner of wild fruits, berries and seeds are eagerly eaten.

The bird in the painting is a female of the red-shafted variety. She sits hunched on a bare apple bough in the winter sunshine, a bulky, strong-featured bird with the characteristic white rump patch clearly in evidence. This is how we usually see them and only when they fly away in their bounding woodpecker fashion do we momentarily glimpse the lovely colours of their wings.

These birds indulge in a very active courtship, beginning with the loud, laughing *wick wick wick wick* call and culminating in sexual flights and a strange-looking dance. Two or more birds begin displaying, either perched close together on a branch or clinging to a tree trunk. They spread their tails, point their bills skyward and start to bow and bob, their heads jerking backward and sideways in a curious weaving motion. The performance goes on for some time to the accompaniment of the subdued *wick-up* notes that are part of it. Sometimes the protagonists break off to pursue each other briefly; now and then there is a mild clash, followed by more posturing and bobbing.

Sooner or later, the matter of mates is decided and the new pairs begin to look for nesting sites. These are almost always holes excavated by the birds in suitable trees. A dead stub will be used or a partly unsound tree, for the decayed wood makes the arduous task of excavation easier. (However some crazy situations have been recorded—wagon wheel hubs, haystacks and even the bare ground. All these have been used by flickers whose discernment must have been defective.)

Laying out the dimensions of the entrance with a few taps the flicker, now all woodpecker, braces its stiff tail and begins to hack out the cavity with pick-like, downward strokes of its bill. Male and female take turns until only the tips of their tails show. At that point they dig downward and carve out a nesting chamber about a foot or eighteen inches below the level of the entrance. The chips are usually carried away and much of the sawdust is swallowed.

Between five and ten eggs are laid on a light lining of chips and sawdust. When the naked young are first hatched they are fed by regurgitation and later on broken-up insects. Their eyes do not open for about ten days but much earlier than that the babies perceive light and shade. According to one account the darkening of the entrance causes them to raise their heads and beg for food. In about three weeks they are strong enough to cling to the walls of their nursery and in a little less than a month they leave it. Once out of the nest they are taught to find their own food and to look for it in likely places. Bringing a tender grub or other tid-bit, the parent tucks it behind a piece of loose bark for the young to retrieve. This is repeated until the young one catches on.

In suburban areas flickers are familiar visitors to feeders. Most other birds make way for them and even starlings are usually kept at bay, but they have been less successful in keeping these pushy aliens out of their nests. Starlings nest in holes, too, and wild battles between these two species have been witnessed. Usually the starlings are victorious, for they call in reinforcements and drive the flickers away. Flickers have more direct enemies such as Cooper's hawks and others who enjoy a woodpecker meal.

33 Red-breasted Sapsucker

Sphyrapicus varius ruber

Ornithologically speaking, the red-breasted sapsucker has had a rather up and down history during the last hundred years. At one time or another it has been either a full species or a mere subspecies of the yellow-bellied sapsucker, according to the prevailing opinions of eminent scientists. The current thought, I believe, is that the birds are too closely allied to be considered as separate species and that our beautiful red-breasted sapsucker is but a western race.

Individual birds are found mid-way between the two varieties but in its typical plumage the whole head and chest of the western form is a deep, lovely red. In fall and winter, after the moult, the red is somewhat darker while it attains its brightest shade in summer when the feathers have become abraded through wear.

A somewhat specialized group of woodpeckers, the sapsuckers owe their curious name (which has been such a rich source of amusement to non-bird people), to a well-developed habit of tapping trees for the sap. Using their chisel bills they cut the outer bark in strips or in a vertical series of squarish perforations to expose the cambrium layer and reach the sweet, exuding fluid. Many kinds of trees—A.C. Bent says at least sixty-seven—are treated in this way including apple, pear and other orchard varieties. Working downward so as to always have a fresh flow, the birds make their wells and thereafter pay regular visits to them, each to its own. Much time is spent by the sapsuckers simply resting nearby, guarding the wells or perhaps contemplating their own ingenuity. There is reason for guarding, because the flow of juice attracts not only other woodpeckers, which are chased away, but different birds such as warblers and also, of course, many insects. Fruit-growers look askance, knowing well that a regularly tapped tree may suffer considerable damage through bleeding or because of its increased susceptibility to insect pests and disease.

Red-breasted sapsuckers also eat the cambrium itself, but balancing this, and to some extent the sap-sipping propensity which brings them into disrepute with orchardists, is their consumption of injurious insects. Many harmful beetles and larvae are devoured, especially when young birds are being fed at the nest. Ants form a major part of the sapsucker's food though most other birds find these too bitter to the taste.

As spring approaches, the red-breasted sapsucker, in the manner of woodpeckers, becomes more noticeable. The resonant drumming of the males and their calls can be heard in places frequented by these birds. They have no specially preferred habitat and their bright, flashing forms may be glimpsed in aspen groves, among streamside willows or in the firs and pines of hillsides. In winter they come more often into towns; a few years ago on our coldest recorded December day I saw one hunched at the base of a redwood in a city park. On lower Vancouver Island I have not found this bird to be very plentiful. Though one comes across their rows of drilling on trees, the birds remain elusive.

Nesting cavities are cut out at a goodly height from the ground, very often in live trees but also in decayed or dead stubs. The digging is a protracted business, taking a week or more to complete particularly in trees that are healthy. The typically white eggs of a hole-nesting species, five to seven in number, are laid in a bed of fine chips. As long as they remain in the dark and narrow nest the young are fed a high-protein diet of caterpillars and other larvae, grubs and insects. Only later do the parents introduce them to the delights of the rising sap and apparently some pains are taken to properly instruct the offspring.

Sapsuckers seem to move about in the fall and winter, perhaps down to the lower levels in an irregular altitudinal migration if the weather is inclement. However, through most of its range up and down the west coast, there seems to be no definite exodus at summer's end or corresponding return in spring. At any time of the year one may come across this beautiful, remarkable bird. Most often, with feathers fluffed and crimson foreparts glowing, it will be hanging quietly against the trunk of a tree, silent and easily overlooked.

34 Western Flycatcher

Empidonax difficilis

Each spring I wait to hear the jaunty, penetrating *pi-séet* that announces the first western flycatcher. Late April or early May sees the arrival in the northwest of this bird, for which I have a special regard. Its cheering, up-beat call, small size and slender, softly-coloured presence give it an engaging air.

Western flycatchers do not suffer from the narrow consistency that affects many birds in their choice of building sites and this catholicity of taste enables them to nest in a wide variety of places. The first nest I found was at Prospect Lake on Vancouver Island. A pair had built on the back porch of a cabin in which my family stayed for a time and there I made what may have been my first drawing of birds from life. I still have it in an old notebook, showing only the head and tail of the incubating parent projecting over the rim of the nest.

Beams of porches and outbuildings are frequently used by western flycatchers, and having found a place to their liking they and their successors will return to it again and again. The anchoring fork of an alder branch or some other tree is a typical location but nests have been found in stream banks, in holes and on stumps—anywhere that will serve as a base. The little edifice itself is a pretty sight, built of moss gathered from tree trunks and from the ground. In this pliant mass a nesting cup or depression is formed to hold the three or four eggs and this is lined with soft inner bark fibres, often of cedar, the reddish colour contrasting nicely with the green, freshly-gathered moss.

This bird may be recognized as a flycatcher by its actions, for it captures its prey in the typical manner of the family—darting from its perch and returning after snapping up a passing insect; from a little distance the click of its bill is clearly audible. Small wasps and flies make up much of its food.

As well as the distinctive call that proclaims its identity to the uncertain observer, the western flycatcher has a song of sorts. It is a simple affair of three or four notes arranged in phrases and repeated continuously. The phrases are not always complete and the notes may be scrambled and rearranged to suit the singer's inclination. There is also a short alarm note. This is one of a group of little greenish-grey flycatchers collectively called by their generic name *Empidonax*. In the field they are virtually indistinguishable one from the other and though each is generally restricted to its own favourite habitat, the safest way to tell them apart is by voice.

The western flycatcher does not bear the specific name *difficilis* for nothing, but though it is so like others in the group, it does have yellower underparts and buffier wing-bars than some. Too, it is a little less exclusive in its choice of surroundings and may be found anywhere provided that large deciduous trees are nearby. It does not care for coniferous woods.

Its real preference, however, is for bottom land where groves of alder, dogwood or maple have formed near streams or ponds. In such quiet woodland scenes, where little bird-song breaks the stillness, the voice of this flycatcher is a familiar sound through the summer months.

By the third week in September it has left the more northerly parts of its range for a warmer climate where insects are plentiful.

35 Violet-green Swallow

Tachycineta thalassina

Westerners are fortunate to have this beautiful species as a familiar summer resident of their garden nesting boxes. It is, in the northwest at least, almost exclusively a bird of the settlements and has largely forsaken its ancestral habitat. Here it is the earliest swallow to arrive in spring and to winter-dampened humans its first appearance brings an inevitable cheering and happy anticipation of summer's warm and easy days.

People grown accustomed to seeing this swallow about the towns and who always see it from below may be surprised, upon looking at the painting, to see how handsome it is. Unlike the other green and white species, the tree swallow, whose dorsal surface has a gun-metal glint, the upper parts of this bird are of two soft but vivid greens divided at the nape by a blue and violet band. The snowy face and rump patches not only make a very nice contrast but serve to distinguish it from its relative.

The violet-green swallow winters far south, as far as Guatemala and Costa Rica. Very early in spring it appears along the North American west coast and usually the first of the returning migrants reach Vancouver Island in mid-February and not later than March.

Upon arrival in their general breeding area, they never come immediately into the suburbs but confine themselves to the outlying countryside. Wary and seemingly distrustful of man and his proximity, they can be found in flocks hawking low over the lakes and meadows. Their presence is uncertain at first and after being around for a day they may disappear in an apparent retreat. Most likely the flocks pass on, leaving a vacuum until their place is taken by the next advancing wave. In town, it is not until the first days of April that one hears the first twittering overhead and sees, at a considerable height, the chunky form of a swallow.

This species occurs throughout the west in summer from Alaska to lower California and though it shares much of its range with the tree swallow, it largely preempts the latter in populated areas. On Vancouver Island one loses the violet-green as one leaves the towns but elsewhere it is as much a bird of the wilderness as any other. There it readily breeds in natural crevices in rocky country as well as in cavities in dead trees. One pair of town swallows does not care to nest near another, but in more natural surroundings they may breed in colonies and the pairs may be cheek-by-jowl where suitable building sites are few.

Prospecting for nests seems to take some time. Two or three weeks pass before the swallows make their selection and it is some time again before building begins. I have seen the female, who seems to choose the home, spend several days passing and repassing a likely spot. She comes closer each time until finally alighting at the entrance for an inspection.

The nest cavity is filled with grass and straws and a good many feathers, the whole forming a somewhat untidy but comfortable bed for the three or four young that are hatched. Violet-greens suffer, to some extent, from persecution by house sparrows wherever the two species come in contact, the swallows usually coming off second best. Sparrows owe some of their advantage to being residents and to the male's habit of taking possession in winter of the home that he and his mate will occupy in spring. By the time the swallows arrive many desirable nesting places are taken. Sparrows also attempt active eviction of the violet-greens and anyone desiring the latter's presence and wishing to discourage the former should make the holes of nest boxes one inch or slightly less in diameter. This will prevent house sparrows in most cases from gaining entrance.

The young are out of the nest in about twenty-three days and by the end of June most of the season's crop of swallows is on the wing and flying strongly. There is no great preparation with them, no chattering rows of restless migrants lining the wires as in the case of departing barn swallows. From the northern part of their range they begin to slip unobtrusively away early in July and before the end of that month I look up and realize, always with surprise, that the swallows have gone—the skies will be empty of them for another eight months.

36 Steller's Jay
Cyanocitta stelleri

This long-crested, black-fronted bird is the western counterpart of the blue jay. Though unalike in appearance, the two species share many family traits, both being rude, raucous birds with quick wits and what might be described as a sense of humour.

One of several races of a species that occupies a range from Alaska to Nicaragua and from the Rocky Mountains to the Pacific, Steller's jay is the variety found on the northwest coast. The first specimen brought to European attention was collected by Steller, the naturalist of Vitus Bering's northern expedition in the eighteenth century. Later he was honoured by having this species of jay named after him. His name is well known in the north, and not only the jay but an eider and two arctic mammals, the sea lion and the now extinct sea-cow, also bear his name.

I know the Steller's jay as a bird of the conifers where one is often glimpsed as it climbs from branch to branch, spiral-fashion around a fir, pausing at the top to scream its jay-scream before taking flight.

Food is a variety of things. Like others in the crow family, jays do their share of nest robbing and camp thievery. In the autumn, parties wander into orchards and farmland to seek what they can find in the way of fruit or waste grain. Near Victoria they sometimes come to the Garry oaks for the acorns, which are buried or stored away in holes and crannies for possible winter reference.

Jay populations seem to fluctuate, building to large numbers every few years. Perhaps this coincides with good food years that allow a successful raising of more young than usual. Whatever the reason, suddenly there are too many jays and, overflowing the woods, they come into the towns and are seen as commonly as crows in every suburban garden. Even the most inattentive person cannot help noticing the strident cries and colours of the invaders.

The nest is large and coarse—a deep mud cup lined with rootlets, the whole structure on a bulky base of twigs. Here, ten to forty feet up on a fir branch, are laid the greenish eggs, generally four though sometimes three or five. The parents become very secretive at this time, moving silently to and fro.

In those spring and summer weeks they are surprisingly hard to see and though in later months they become bolder, still it is only when a jay comes into the open that the dark bird turns and one sees, as bright as a gas flame, the blue of wings and tail. Because the coloration is prismatic and not due to pigment in the feathers, it varies with light source and intensity, changing from violet to pale cerulean. This becomes the despair of any painter trying to put the shade on paper.

The usual call is a harsh and rasping *chaak! chaak!*, not as nasal as the blue jay's tin-trumpet note but unmistakably "jay-made." I have heard one singing a soft sweet whisper-song while exploring the ground and bushes of my garden; other observers have heard this occasionally, too. In addition there is the usual range of mimic calls and noises. Theed Pearse of Comox described to author A.C. Bent hearing one imitating a crow's spring song and another uttering a strong, warbling song of its own which he thought "delightful." A scream like that of a red-tailed hawk is heard, too.

There seems to be no definite or large-scale migration; the jays simply travel about in small bands or families in the winter, going where food supplies take them rather than in any particular direction.

I remember first seeing Steller's jays, in what must have been one of their years of abundance; on that fall afternoon they became part of one of my most vivid childhood experiences. Near Mill Bay, where we lived at the time, a line of walnut trees and a split-cedar fence ran along the edge of a field. There, six years old, I stood with my mother as several jays peered at us from the low branches of the walnuts. Surprisingly, they made no sound and had no fear, for they came very close to us and even a squirrel on the fence was so approachable that we could see the parasites on its fur.

The jays, the squirrel and a sapsucker above us would have affected me at any time but the silence and tameness of the creatures that day stirred me deeply and made all seem enchanted. Now, when driving on the highway past the still-standing trees, I look across with the eyes of thirty years ago and in my mind see the jays that from that day on have always been birds of excitement and beauty.

37 Chestnut-backed Chickadee

Parus rufescens

Who does not know the chickadee? In all parts of Canada and the United States it is the hardy visitor to winter feeding stations and its sociable manner and wheezy, breezy call make it everyone's favourite.

There are several kinds of chickadees and throughout most of North America the black-capped is most familiar. On the west coast, in a narrow and rather restricted range extending barely a hundred miles inland at its widest point, lives our own handsome chestnut-backed chickadee. It is well known to any coast-dweller between Alaska and California and to people inland in one or two places where it appears in isolated pockets of suitable country.

On the mainland edge it shares its range with the black-capped chickadee but holds for itself the outlying islands, to the exclusion of other chickadee species. Here it may be found in almost any kind of country—in the roadside bushes, among deciduous trees and in suburban gardens where it works its way through the apple trees and shrubbery, hanging, swinging, examining every leaf, top and bottom, for tiny insects.

Strictly speaking, this is a bird of heavy timber and it is truly at home in the dense forests of fir and cedar and pine. In this kind of country where bird sounds are few, and what sounds there are come down from the canopy high above, the *dee dee* notes of the chestnut-backed chickadee are heard. Often a party of a dozen or so will descend to the branches nearer ground level and then are found to be travelling, not alone, but in the company of a regular band of companions. Almost always among them will be golden-crowned kinglets, their high notes thinly filling the air. One or two red-breasted nuthatches will be *hank-hanking* nasally on the periphery of the group, and also perhaps a single creeper whose sibilant note is so high as to be almost inaudible. Together they work their way through the forest, the chickadees and kinglets coming with indifference within a foot or two of the observer's face. They move on, their medley of calls fading as they pass.

In these gypsy bands of little birds the chickadees seem almost robust when compared with the fluttering kinglets. They seem oblivious to human presence, or at least unconcerned, but I have the impression that they are a little wilder and less confiding than the black-cap. I have not seen them come to the hand as other species so readily do and while they are unafraid, chestnut-backed chickadees preserve their independence.

All of the chickadee group build nests in cracks and cavities of dead trees and this species is no exception. A limb or part of a tree split or cracked by frost or disease, riven by lightning or simply decayed through age, makes an admirable home for a pair of chickadees. They build low, seldom more than five or ten feet from the ground, but because such a small bird needs only the slimmest aperture to its chamber the nest may be overlooked quite easily.

The newly-hatched young are, of course, without feathering and it takes about sixteen days for them to fledge, grow and leave the nest. There are usually six or seven of them and when they emerge into the outside world they are almost exactly like their parents, although a little smaller and softer. At the end of the breeding season the plumage of the parents is somewhat worn and the young seen in company with them have much whiter and fresher cheeks. The moult of late summer puts the matter right and replaces the tattered and abraded feathers of the adults.

Throughout the year the mainstay of the chestnut-backed chickadee is insect life but in winter, when animal food is harder to come by, it is supplemented to some extent by wild fruits and other vegetarian fare. In addition, the coconuts, peanut butter and suet of feeding stations all help to keep out the cold, and are accepted with alacrity.

Chickadees are hardy birds, quite able to withstand most degrees of cold weather. Furthermore, the climate of the west coast is not usually severe and so there is no need for any regular migration.

38 Bewick's Wren

Thryomanes bewickii

One does not have to go far to find a Bewick's wren. It does not object to the proximity of people and in rural or suburban districts it is an everyday "dooryard" bird. Away from man, it prefers brushy patches and open woodland edges, avoiding the deep forest that is the winter wren's chosen home.

This species has a fairly wide distribution in North America and occurs all along the west coast as far north as Vancouver Island and southwestern British Columbia. To some extent it has expanded its range northward during this century and in many areas it seems to replace the house wren near human habitation. The two do not get along well together and I suspect the Bewick's wren, being a little larger and perhaps more aggressive, pushes the latter out of the way whenever they meet. In any event, they are not happy in company.

Small birds search endlessly for sustenance during their waking hours and none pursues the search with such peering, prying intensity as a Bewick's wren. One or two can usually be found in the garden of my studio. It is very tangled and overgrown but neglect has made it a nice place for birds and the wrens like it. Often when I look up from my drawing board, I see one or two hunting through the clematis on the verandah. They are very thorough. They creep like mice into cracks and openings in the building and under the eaves, their eyes never missing a fly or a small spider. With their curved, probe-like bills they have an air of unusual purpose and persistence.

Bewick's wren is a plump little bird with rather endearing habits. It scolds and chatters with seeming irritability from some place of concealment and when provocation becomes too great, it hops into plain view and continues its tirade. The tail is usually held high but except in moments of great excitement is not carried over the back at an extreme angle in the manner of some wrens.

Its song is sweet, an emphatic melody a little reminiscent of a song sparrow's, but stronger. It can be heard on fine days in winter, though usually in a softer or abbreviated form, and in the fall there is a partial resumption of singing after a few weeks of near-silence.

As the approach of spring generates the well-known feelings in all members of the animal kingdom, these wrens become quite noisy. Courtship induces a lot of chasing and squeaking but the harsh notes are interrupted by sudden and frequent bursts of song as rivals confront each other and dispute the boundaries of their territories. The singing and sexual excitement reaches a peak in May and early June and then declines while the birds are engaged in raising their families. With half-a-dozen or more fledglings to feed there can be little time or energy left for song.

Under natural conditions Bewick's wren will nest in some sort of cavity such as a hole in a stump or perhaps a fissure in a rock or cave. These are the ancestral choices but around humans they choose stranger sites and one may find a nest in the mailbox or in an overturned tin on a shelf. The choices of location seem capricious and are impossible to predict. The nest itself is bulky and untidy. Bits of grass, twigs and moss are stuffed into the given space with the addition of a few feathers as lining.

Between five and seven pretty, brown-speckled eggs are laid and after about fourteen days they hatch into a brood of wide-mouthed, insatiably hungry young birds. In the calculation of one patient observer who watched a family of Bewick's wrens, they are fed on an average of every 3.04 minutes throughout the day. The hard-pressed parents must bring tremendous quantities of caterpillars and other insects to quell the appetites, for in such tiny bodies food is assimilated very quickly.

During the two weeks they remain in the nest, the young grow rapidly. At the end of that time, when they leave, they have changed from blind, naked things to stumpy-tailed duplicates of their elders. They must still be fed for another two weeks after that and when these babies are old enough to look after themselves, the parents begin again and raise a second family.

The wren in the painting is perched on a nightshade plant that I found growing in profusion over a railway loading platform. It was tangled and entwined with a clematis and it is in just such a setting—impenetrable, confused creepers and half-decayed building—that one is most likely to hear the rasping voice of a Bewick's wren.

39 Varied Thrush

Ixoreus naevius

The varied thrush is truly a bird of the Pacific rain forest; none, not even Steller's jay, is a more characteristic inhabitant of this dark, primeval land.

In the moss-hung, immense forests where mist blots the hillsides, the wild, extraordinary voice of this thrush is a haunting and mysterious element. The song is remarkable, a series of five long, vibrant notes delivered slowly in different keys and in any order. At close range a sixth note and a harsh sound are sometimes heard. There is something of the flute-like timbre common to many thrush voices but the song is unlike any other; heard in its proper setting it has an unearthly quality that is quite moving. Many have heard the subdued but penetrating notes without knowing the identity of their author, for the varied thrush is a retiring bird that blends admirably with its surroundings.

Its summer home is, for the most part, at higher elevations near the coast, where fir, spruce and cedar surround mountain lakes. Toward the southern part of its range in California I believe it is found sometimes among live oaks and willows, though even there it prefers the misty, fern-clad canyon sides.

Normally it is only in cold weather that townsmen see this thrush. The "winter robin" always attracts attention and as a child, if there came a heavy fall of snow, I would watch eagerly for the first varied thrush, something I still do today. A harsh winter drives them down to the more hospitable environs of human settlements where otherwise they would not venture. The splendid plumage of the males, underlit so beautifully by the snow, and their wild, elusive air make them exotic visitors to a winter garden.

They will come reluctantly to the feeder with other birds, giving way to starlings and aggressive robins. They are less timid when offered apples. One season some of my apples fell and were left to lie under the trees, and later many thrushes came with the robins to hungrily devour the frozen and fermenting fruit. Puffed out with the cold, the birds in their plumages of rich autumnal colours made a beautiful combination with the russets and yellows of the apples.

The nest, in a young fir, perhaps, or a hemlock, is seldom more than ten or fifteen feet from the ground and is built on a support of small branches against the tree trunk. As bulky as a robin's nest, it has an exterior of moss, leaves and twigs, often with an inner layer of smoothly-shaped leaf mould from the forest floor. The cup which will contain the spotted, pale blue eggs is softly formed of fine grasses. Of course, the material used is not always the same and the site, too, may vary from a high outer branch to the ground itself.

A full clutch may be three eggs or, just as often, as many as five. After they have hatched, the young, like those of almost all songbirds, are fed a diet of insects. Because the adults are mostly ground feeders, flicking over the leaf mould and jumping back to expose things underneath, the nestlings get a lot of millepedes, daddy-long-legs and isopods (those grey armadillo creatures that some children call "roll-ups"). However, in fall and winter the thrushes feed on wild berries and fruit, together with different seeds. Juvenile varied thrushes in their first year are pale editions of their parents, most closely resembling the mature females. Whereas the male adults are slate blue, black-banded and fiery orange below, the females and young are softly brown above with underparts pale amber and chest bands often so light as to be barely noticeable.

There is a fairly strong migration at the extreme limits of the breeding range but at the centre, in any event on Vancouver Island, thrushes are to be seen throughout the year. Perhaps those that breed here stay here or possibly their place is taken in winter by birds from the north.

40 Hermit Thrush

Hylocichla guttata

There is something about a thrush, something elusively subtle in its air of wildness and its delicate form, that sets it apart from other birds. The wistful, seemingly sad expression in the liquid dark of its eye and its shy demeanor are to me compellingly attractive. This spirit or essence, not easily expressed in words, is still harder to capture in a painting, and I have always found thrushes the most difficult songbirds to portray successfully.

Some species have exquisite songs. At the maple-hung lip of an incredible Catskill gorge I have listened in silent admiration to the fluting of a woodthrush and many times in the Cowichan Valley I have heard rising from the riverside alder thickets the ethereal choir of the Swainson's thrushes. Each of these experiences has moved me, and yet, fine as the others are, the song of the hermit thrush transcends all. The purity and spirituality conveyed by its vocal expression make the hermit the finest singer of all our birds. It ranks with and perhaps even surpasses its European relative, the fabled nightingale.

All who attempt a description of its song turn eventually to a religious idiom and to do so is natural and inevitable, for belief in a Creator seems implicit in the phrases of this small bird's song. As the incomparable notes reach the listener they become a vesper hymn and the still, twilit forest a vaulted cathedral. One must go to the north woods to know the hermit thrush in its most natural and typical setting. There in the pre-dawn, and again at sunset of the spring days soon after arriving, it pours out its heart.

Several races of hermit thrush occur in the west, some a little greyer or smaller or darker than others but indistinguishable to the observer. In late fall hermits appear on the west coast and are seen for a week or two in the countryside and in town gardens. These are thrushes that have bred in northern British Columbia and Alaska, rather dark birds of two northern races which at this time of year are moving southward to their wintering grounds in California.

I see them on the lawns in Victoria around November—slender, almost silent birds moving over the grass rather in the manner of robins. They run a few steps, stop and run again with wings drooped and rufous tails raised at an angle. A useful point in identification is the contrast between the reddish tails and the umber backs. So, too, is the slow elevation of the tails upon alighting and constant, rapid flirting of the wings.

The hermit thrushes reappear in spring and we may hear occasionally a soft whisper song—the barest hint or foreshadowing of the full-throated melody of a week or two later. To hear it one must be close, for this sub-song is faint and audible for only a short distance.

Hermit thrushes are ground-nesters. Choosing a little depression or protected spot at the base of a tree they construct a firm, bulky nest from moss, leaves and small sticks—a common enough kind of thrush nest. The incubating bird and her mate come and go with caution, for a family raised on the ground is especially liable to discovery and disaster.

The breeding season is long, from the beginning of May until late in August, the hermit thrushes being hardy birds in no hurry to leave their summer homes. This protracted season means that at least two broods can be raised, a factor which helps counteract the high incidence of mortality suffered by the nestlings. Three to six eggs are laid and when the young hatch after some twelve days of incubation the solicitous parents at once begin bringing the little green larvae that are a nestling's staff of life. Many other insects are brought too: as the babies grow, the size of the food increases and grasshoppers, large moths and caterpillars are offered to nearly fledged nestlings before they leave.

As adults, hermit thrushes in the summer months feed extensively on the myriad insects about them as well as on worms and little ground-dwelling things of the forest floor. In autumn and winter when these are not so easily found, they turn to the abundant fruits and berries that ripen so providently.

The long flights made by migrants are hazardous journeys, undertaken at night and, for the young birds, through unfamiliar country. For birds such as hermit thrushes and other small species that travel at low levels they are particularly perilous. A season seldom passes without my finding several thrushes and fox sparrows dead on the streets and boulevards; in the dark they have collided with the unseen power lines strung at fatal height. The bird whose portrait I have painted was such a victim. In this likeness once again he flits, inquisitive and alert, to the exposed tip of a dead branch.

41 Hutton's Vireo

Vireo huttoni

Vireos are unobtrusive little birds. Though not unlike heavy-bodied fall warblers in appearance, they lack the warblers' intensity and sprightly activity. Both groups feed on tiny insects but whereas warblers are never still, flitting, darting, snatching at passing flies, vireos take life more calmly. They are content to examine the leaves and twigs in a slow and leisurely fashion, picking here and there at the things they find.

Nondescript in colouring—most of them are greenish grey or yellowish olive —and somewhat sluggish in habits, vireos are difficult to see and are therefore easily overlooked. One may stand gazing at a bush or tree for minutes at a time, hearing but unable to find the singer.

In the Pacific northwest, Hutton's vireo is a bird of second growth coniferous forest and shrubby edges—though farther south in California it is known almost exclusively as an inhabitant of the live oaks. Its distribution in summer and winter varies little as there is no migration to speak of. In the northwest where it is found west of the Cascade Mountains and into southwestern British Columbia, it is the only member of its family to remain throughout the winter.

As I was painting this vireo I was struck by its resemblance to a ruby-crowned kinglet. True, the kinglet is smaller and rounder but otherwise they are remarkably alike with the same eye-ring and wing-bars, the same colouring above and below. A careless observer or one unfamiliar with the birds of the area might easily confuse one with the other. The possible confusion between the two is compounded when the vireo, as it often does in fall and winter, joins the wandering gangs of kinglets and chickadees that travel about the countryside with their following of miscellaneous other species.

Hutton's vireo is a quiet bird and is silent much of the time—but it does have a simple call note and becoming familiar with this is the best way of finding the bird. Its song is uncomplicated though not unpleasing; a rapid, protracted repetition of two notes, often continuing for several minutes.

Vireos generally make rather beautiful nests and that of Hutton's vireo is an attractive structure built of *Usnea*, the wispy, hanging lichen, and has a soft lining of grasses. Taking the form of a deep cup, the nest is anchored securely across a branch fifteen to twenty feet or more above the ground. The material of which it is composed, its concealed location and neat construction make it difficult for even a predator to discover. Nevertheless, it is not always proof against the persistent cowbird. Recently I was told of a Hutton's vireo nest found containing the single egg of a cowbird together with those of the rightful inhabitants. The egg was removed but the cowbird returned to lay two more, whereupon the exasperated vireos abandoned the project and site altogether.

42 Orange-crowned Warbler

Vermivora celata

This is one of the commonest and most frequently seen warblers on the Pacific coast, particularly in the northwest. It is inconspicuously coloured and without much distinction, though the race occurring on the coast is brighter and yellower than those found elsewhere. The very absence of any distinguishing features is in itself a good field-mark of the orange-crowned warbler.

The bright race of the northwest is known locally as the "lutescent warbler," one of the many sub-specific names of birds that were once in general use but are now being abandoned. The specific name Orange-crowned refers to an almost hidden patch of burnt-orange on top of this otherwise soberly-clad bird's head. This patch is almost never visible to us, being concealed by the olive-grey feather tips most of the time. Occasionally in the right light it shows faintly, especially near summer's end when the edges of the feathers have worn away.

The lutescent is one of our first breeding warblers to arrive in spring. The myrtle is an earlier migrant, flitting high in the still-bare branches in March or the first days of April, but close behind it presses the lutescent. Its song—a simple rising and then more slowly descending trill—is heard when few other birds have begun to sing. About the end of April I heard this warbler's little cascade of notes in the Garry oaks around Victoria; at that time of year there is little chance of confusing this species with another, for yellow warblers and black-capped are still on their way and the autumn confusion of look-alike warblers is far ahead.

This is one of the ground-nesting warblers. It builds a well-concealed home that may be in a clump of dead leaves caught at the base of a bush. Sometimes it will be placed on a small tangled bank or in the protection afforded by a fallen tree, or at other times sheltered beneath an upturned root. It is made of moss and leaves, bits of grass and ferns and lined with soft grasses. A feather or two may be included and some hair if that material is available. The whole is artfully incorporated into the fallen leaves and natural debris so as to escape detection. Usually about four eggs are laid (though there may be as many as six), matte white with dark speckles and scrawls.

In late August the warblers begin their fall migration. The young of the year are in their first, rather drab plumage, and the adults of many species have assumed a more sombre appearance than in spring. As birds that have bred to the north of us begin to trickle past, we are confronted by many warblers, all more or less yellow and all bewilderingly alike.

43 Wilson's Warbler

Wilsonia pusilla

This small, attractive bird has borne more than one long name in its scientific history. The one in general use today is Wilson's warbler, after the nineteenth century Scottish-American naturalist. However, "pileolated" and "black-capped" are alternative appellations that have been applied to it by ornithologists.

Whatever you call it, Wilson's warbler is a handsome bird. As with the orange-crowned warbler, the Pacific race is particularly brightly coloured, the yellow being a rich, golden shade. It is always a pleasure to see one of these plump, fussy little insect-eaters, with its olive back and chrome yellow underparts, the neat black cap set squarely on its head. It behaves very like a kinglet, for it is in constant motion, fluttering up and darting out at passing flies. These tell-tale actions, useful in identification, are so characteristic of its behaviour that they gave rise to yet another name: the "black-capped fly-catching warbler."

At the height of the spring migration a party of black-caps may arrive together and as they feed in the shrubbery of parks and gardens their sprightly ways and golden plumage make a pretty sight. At this time, early May, they are on their way to breeding grounds beyond us, perhaps north as far as the Yukon, and they are in full song. Their notes are much like a yellow warbler's but weaker and without the energetic delivery.

The Wilson's is a warbler of the underbrush and the lower strata of deciduous trees, seldom being seen more than ten or fifteen feet from the ground. In the northwest we see it mostly in passage, when it may be found in a variety of places. Its summer retreats, however, are alder stands, damp and mossy woods and sphagnum bogs. These are the secluded places frequented by this bird in the breeding season, where it lays four to six eggs and raises its family.

The nest is on the ground, sunk into a deep moss cushion, perhaps at the base of a small tree. I have not seen one, but the nest is composed of moss, leaves and grass, quite bulky and larger than those of other ground-nesting warblers. All accounts of this bird at the nest mention its remarkable tameness and its refusal to be intimidated or frightened away by human intruders. After being flushed from the nest it will reappear almost at once, often perching on the person standing in the way of its parental duties.

44 Audubon's Warbler

Dendroica coronata auduboni

The Audubon's warbler, yellow-throated, and the similar myrtle warbler with its white throat, are now recognized as one. The "new" species has been given the devastatingly prosaic name of "yellow-rumped warbler" but those who regret the passing of the old, romantic names and their associations can take heart in the knowledge that they are still in use to differentiate between the two forms.

Generally speaking, Audubon's warbler is a western bird and the myrtle an eastern one, but in some places their ranges coincide and on the west coast in very early spring there is a migration of both varieties. They are the first warbler migrants to appear and as they flit by in March and April, one must look carefully to tell one from the other.

Audubon's warbler has a breeding range that extends less far to the north than the myrtle's and farther south to California, Arizona and western Texas. In summer, Audubon's warbler is distinctly a mountain bird, breeding to elevations of ten thousand feet or more above sea level. It is plentiful all through the zones of pine and fir almost to the timber limit where the trees begin to stunt and fail. It is one of the few warblers to be encountered at these heights, and against the dark foliage of the evergreens its handsome and brightly varied plumage shows to advantage.

In fall, Audubon's warblers descend to the more temperate lowlands. They are hardy birds but suffer when faced with prolonged or severe cold and in September there begins a strong migratory movement southward.

In subdued autumnal plumage they appear along the Pacific coast in considerable numbers, travelling in flocks and often associating with other birds. On Vancouver Island, should one now be lucky enough to come across a party of western bluebirds, it is almost certain that Audubon's warblers will be in attendance. As the bluebirds with their gentle, muted voices perch on fenceposts and wires, the warblers flicker and dart in the roadside bushes.

The colouring of Audubon's warbler is brightest in spring when the males are most strikingly marked with black breasts, blue-grey backs and flashes of white on wings and tails. Females and young bear fine yellow patches but the whole plumage is duller and browner, much like that of the autumn male depicted here. The yellow crown is not always visible as the surrounding feathers may partly conceal it and the birds usually are above an observer's head.

The nests are prettily constructed of small branches with finer twigs forming the interior. Most often the nesting cup is lined with rootlets and feathers; should the large, soft feathers of gallinaceous birds be used, they arch over the cup in an attractive manner and partially cover the four eggs. The site chosen is generally an evergreen tree in which the nest is placed thirty feet or more above the forest floor.

Fall migration takes most of these warblers from us, but not uncommonly a few winter on the coast, particularly if the season is mild. In a place where the winter birds are drab, an Audubon's warbler in the bare January rose bushes provides a vivid and welcome spark of colour.

45 Townsend's Warbler

Dendroica townsendi

Few people are acquainted with this bright-plumaged inhabitant of the western forests; its drowsy *wheezy-wheezy-wheezy-whee* drifts down from above but the singer remains all but hidden in the thick-crowned firs. It moves restlessly through the upper foliage, pausing only briefly to snap up a weevil or fly before hurrying onward in its ceaseless, far-ranging search for food.

Arriving rather late—sometime in May—Townsend's warblers are found commonly in summer wherever there is suitable forest, from Washington north as far as Alaska. During most of their time with us they are tree-top birds, remaining high in the tallest of the conifers. There they forage and sing and mate many feet above the ground, seldom descending to anywhere near our level. To see them we must stand with necks uncomfortably craned and with eyes fixed uncertainly on the upper branches.

It is thought that Townsend's warblers often build their nests high in the conifers where they spend so much of their time, though nests no more than ten feet from the ground have been discovered. They are well made of small twigs, plant fibres and cedar bark, are rather shallow in form and are anchored athwart the branches instead of in crotches or forks.

Later in the season these warblers do move a little lower and then may be seen sometimes in smaller second growth and in deciduous trees. This is especially true during their fall and spring migration when their choice of terrain is quite different. When travelling, they take a course through lowland woods, skirting the shores of lakes or following streams. The spring migration is a strong one with successive waves of warblers, males in high plumage and full song, moving northward. Until they reach their ultimate destinations they eschew the forested heights that will later be the chosen haunts of summer.

In the southern part of their breeding range a few Townsend's warblers remain in winter and in California they appear commonly as winter visitors. The main body of birds, however, passes down the coast to Mexico and Central America; in the highlands of Guatemala Townsend's warblers congregate in great numbers and are among the most abundant species during our winter.

46 MacGillivray's Warbler

Oporornis tolmiei

The first intimation of summer's impending death and the approach of fall comes to me with the sharp, stone-against-stone *tchik!* of a MacGillivray's warbler. Even when August is but half gone and the warm days linger as if meaning to stay forever, this bird has read the signs and is on the move. It is the first migrant warbler to come to us from the northern summer, leaving early to begin an astonishing journey that carries it beyond the shores of our continent to the Guatemalan highlands, in Colombia and El Salvador.

MacGillivray's warbler ranges in its breeding season over much of the west, from southeastern Alaska to Montana and New Mexico and parts of California. On the western side of the Rockies it takes the place of the mourning warbler, an eastern bird closely resembling it in habits and appearance. Both species stay near the ground, dwelling in a world bounded a few feet above them by the tops of low bushes growing in their preferred habitats. The home of MacGillivray's warbler lies in tangles of salal, blackberry or thimbleberry, in rank streamside growths of willow or in the brushy confusion of burnt forest where, in the sudden sunlight, new plants spring up to cover the raw earth and fallen trees.

In places like these, the shy and quietly elusive warbler lives out its life. Travelling north in spring, having left the undergrowth of tropical mountainsides, it reaches the woods of our North American west where it sings and courts its mate and raises the four or five young. A foot or so from the ground and perhaps built among the wiry stems of a salal bush, the nest is composed of dried weed stems and grass, with the odd leaf bound into the fabric. This nursery is effectively concealed and may have a partial cover that hides the eggs and young when the parent is away.

The song of this warbler is distinctive, having three or four notes the same, followed by the same number in a lower key: *tee tee tee — chew chew chew.* When the onerous tasks of nesting and feeding fledglings are past, the tattered feathers of the breeding season are shed and a new plumage is assumed, less conspicuous than that worn in spring. The hood, iron-grey in males, is replaced by one of a lighter shade scarcely contrasting with the olive back. In young birds and females it is hardly noticeable and the throat is so pale as to be ashy-white. It is difficult at this time to tell them from the orange-crowned warblers that overtake the stragglers a week or two later, following the same course.

This attractive warbler is known sometimes as Tolmie's warbler for in its Latin appellation it carries the name of Mr. Tolmie, a Hudson's Bay Company factor who showed kindness to naturalists visiting the west. It was thus named by Dr. Townsend but Audubon, acting independently, gave it the name of his Scottish friend in Edinburgh who had been so helpful in the writing of Audubon's *Ornithological Biographies.* Each of these gentlemen, so long departed, would be pleased that his name has been retained and is still borne in one language or the other by this beautiful and interesting bird.

47 Brewer's Blackbird

Euphagus cyanocephalus

Brewer's blackbirds are inhabitants of open country, preferably with marshland or farmland fields. These birds are at home where forests are absent or where at their edge a shrubby growth of bushes is punctuated by isolated trees. The dry click of their voices as scattered flocks pass over is a characteristic sound of the west, from the coast to a point more than halfway across the plains. For some reason, the range of Brewer's blackbird has extended toward the east in recent years, while that lover of the swampy northwoods, the rusty blackbird, has moved westward almost to the shores of the Pacific.

Slim-bodied and quick, Brewer's blackbirds often associate with their more stoutly-built relatives, red-winged blackbirds, which to some extent share their habitat preferences. Compared with these, the Brewer's seem jerky and neurotic, an impression that in males is heightened by their pale, staring eyes. Females are unexceptional, clothed as they are in sooty grey, but the shiny spring males are handsome birds. Hard-plumaged and highly polished in greenish-black and glossy purple, they stalk rapidly, heads bobbing, over the ground or perch in inky rows on overhead wires, uttering creaky notes as metallic as their plumage.

In fall and winter, blackbirds flock together, drifting about on arable land where they feed in the bare fields and on the stubble of harvested grain crops. They glean whatever waste grain still lies and also take many insects and their larvae. More often than not they consort with starlings and the red-wings; when they do, the mixed flocks feed in a distinctive way, working over the ground in open formation. As those in the rear intermittently rise and pass over the front ranks for fresh food, they appear in a dark cloud, vanishing as they settle.

Though the winter flocks do not lose their cohesion until later, the members show signs of pairing as early as January. Increasingly, males and females spend time together as couples and with the beginning of the breeding season the group breaks up as the birds disperse. They build their nests in loose, spaced-out colonies of variable size that may contain half-a-dozen or so pairs to the acre.

Brewer's blackbirds seem to have no definite criteria for nest building; no one particular kind of situation is sought nor is there any standard of height. The records show that almost anywhere and anything will do and while some birds choose to nest on the broken tops of trees, others will build on the ground or somewhere in between.

There is evidence that a male and female, once they have formed a bond, remain together as a pair during subsequent breeding seasons. The uncertainties of their lives must preclude this very often but they appear, whenever possible, to rejoin each other after the winter interval of group living. This faithfulness does not rule out, however, a certain degree of polygamy among some of the more adventurous males.

In a neat twig and grass nest made without her mate's assistance, the female lays four to seven eggs. The number is not constant but five or six eggs seems the commonest size of the full clutch. Blackbirds warn away intruders in a shrilly aggressive way, with much clacking.

This, perhaps, is the time of their greatest usefulness to man—when the fledglings are being fed at the nest. Throughout the year, blackbirds consume a great many insects such as caterpillars and "cutworms" but now with ever-hungry nestlings the campaign against crop pests is tremendously increased. Where mormon crickets occur, blackbirds are among their chief persecutors.

These birds and their relatives, the red-winged blackbirds, cowbirds and grackles, are not noted for melodious songs, but rather for the rusty quality of their notes. All sorts of creaky sounds are issued from their throats and the most attractive effort in the repertoire is a burst of extraordinary liquid notes. It is short, and defies accurate description, but I never tire of listening or watching the male bird ruffling his head and contour feathers when singing. This display is largely one of courtship but there are other posturings and threat displays, also, each with its appropriate note or series of notes.

With the onslaught of snow and cold weather the blackbirds move south, returning to the northern breeding areas sometime in April. Their voices are harsh, their plumage and actions convey no delicacy, but their familiarity makes them welcome.

48 Western Tanager

Piranga ludoviciana

The western tanager seems the most unlikely of all the west coast's migrant birds. In Central and South America where the family origins lie, there are numerous species of tanager but this is the only one among them that ranges as far as the northwestern part of our continent. It seems what it is, a fugitive from a tropical landscape, and against the evergreen background of its summer home the brilliant yellow, red and black of the male's plumage is impossibly exotic.

This bird spends the winter in southern Mexico and beyond, but early in April the first groups of returning migrants reach the Gulf Coast of the United States and begin their annual passage toward their forest breeding grounds. On a broad front they spread northward and by mid-May they can be seen in Oregon and Washington State. The dates of their appearances are fairly consistent and on Vancouver Island I look for them about the fifteenth of May. With a little searching they can usually be found. Tanagers are slow and deliberate in their movements and so do not attract attention by their actions. However, bright as they are, it is difficult to overlook the males. Passing through the crowns of the firs they are spectacular and when several are seen together the sight is memorable.

Tanagers' food consists of both insects and fruit. Where the latter is of cultivated varieties, the birds sometimes cause a good deal of trouble to the commercial growers and are very unpopular. A wave of migrating tanagers that happens upon a cherry orchard may linger for a few days and cause heavy damage to the crop. For the most part, isolated instances of this sort are balanced in the eyes of man by the great number of insects that are devoured. Many of these are beetles and ants though occasionally the tanagers fall from grace and take honey bees.

In the summer months western tanagers are well distributed throughout the west from the eastern slopes of the Rocky Mountains to the Pacific coast and as far north as southern Alaska. They are found more frequently at higher elevations than in the lowlands and range through a number of zones from 1500 to as high as 10,000 feet above sea level. They breed in the pine and fir forests and during the time they spend in the north are, in reality, mountain birds. Their bright beauty enhances the dark, sober green of their surroundings.

Until they hatch the male pays no attention to the eggs, leaving their care and incubation entirely to his greenish-yellow mate. Later when there are three to five nestlings to be fed every few minutes he actively assists the female in bringing the caterpillars and other insects that are the necessary protein-rich food of young songbirds.

The older, beautiful name of Louisiana tanager, borne by this bird in earlier days, derived from a romantic chapter of American history. The first specimens were collected by members of the Lewis and Clarke expedition in the vast western tract of land then known as the Louisiana Purchase and bought by the United States from France in 1814.

In what is now Louisiana the bird is not a usual visitor and so its name has been changed. One wishes that the association could have been retained between this lovely species and those times when the west, utterly unknown, was still in its age-old magnificence.

49 Black-headed Grosbeak

Pheucticus melanocephalus

Easterners have the rose-breasted grosbeak, in which very properly they take pride, for it is a handsome bird with a fine, melodious song that enhances the beauty of spring-time woodlands. However, in the west we are just as fortunate in having its counterpart, the black-headed grosbeak, large and richly-coloured, that ranges between the Rockies' eastern slopes and the Pacific seaboard from British Columbia to Mexico.

Grosbeaks are not especially active birds; they are easy to watch as they move slowly among the branches, feeding quietly. Often one remains for some time on a perch in full view. I recall the first one I saw and my pleasure in seeing it—a male resting a few feet from the ground in a thicket of small poplars. He must have arrived not long before because it was about the time they begin to appear in the northwest, mid-May. Around him in the parkland under the Garry oaks the ground was thickly carpeted with the blue-violet of camas and the lingering pink of shooting-stars; that was twenty-five years ago and houses now cover much of the land as thickly as did the flowers. But some land remains untouched and among the oaks and the creek fringe of little poplar saplings there is still the likelihood of glimpsing a grosbeak and hearing its rich, warbling song.

Black-headed grosbeaks tend to frequent damp and brushy places and can be found in willows and alders near water, in stands of poplars and in open woods and edge-land. They are seen more often than elsewhere in the vicinity of water and a high proportion of nests are built in thickets along the banks of streams.

These nests are untidy and ill-made structures, built about ten feet up and put together with slim twigs and with seeming carelessness. The material is loosely woven in, often so loosely that, standing below, you can count the speckled, bluish eggs through the interstices of the floor. In this aspect the nest is reminiscent of the mourning dove's platform which has more holes than sticks.

A little over half of this grosbeak's food is animal matter, consisting of insects, both adult and larvae, and particularly of beetles which form a large percentage. A bird with so big and stout a bill has no trouble dealing with the tough ecto-skeleton and elytra of these creatures. The remainder of the black-headed grosbeak's diet is made up of tree buds, seeds and fruit, wild and cultivated. Where both grosbeaks and cherries are numerous, the birds are not popular with orchard-keepers because of the damage inflicted upon the fruit crops.

In April, grosbeaks moving north from Oaxaca begin to appear in the most southerly parts of their breeding range, though it is a few weeks later that the northern nesters reach their home ground in British Columbia. Males appear a short time in advance of the females and begin singing as soon as they arrive. They seem to have fairly large and well-defined territories for pairs do not nest near one another and any trespassers are vigorously repelled by the residents.

Before the termination of the breeding season the males cease their elaborate, robin-like carolling and in September the birds slip away. In general, there is little overt preparation or gathering before the migration; they leave unnoticed, one by one working their way southward. In the foot-hills those which have nested higher up may flock together in the canyons before their departure but nearer the coast the grosbeaks simply leave.

50 Red Crossbill

Loxia curvirostra

One of the west's most interesting birds is the red crossbill. Nomadic and occasionally abundant, it is a rather specialized passerine that ranges, in one form or another, over the entire coniferous mantle of the northern hemisphere.

Crossbills are much commoner than may be supposed. As they move about the country, the flocks usually remain high in the trees or silhouetted against the brightness of the sky. Under these conditions the bright plumage is not seen and unless one knows the rapid, swooping flight or is familiar with the metallic *pic pic* of these birds, they go unrecognized. I came to know the red crossbill only when I happened upon six or seven bathing and drinking in a puddle. That was at Mill Bay, on Vancouver Island, where I must have often seen them overhead.

The most immediately arresting feature of the crossbill is, of course, its crossed bill. The long, apparently deformed mandibles, in appearance so awkward and unwieldy, are an efficient adaptation that enables the bird to exploit a particular source of food—the well-protected seeds of coniferous trees. With this practical tool, a crossbill twists apart the tough cone scales and deftly extracts the hidden seeds with its tongue.

Crossbills are quite parrot-like; they creep along the branches and over the cones, often hanging upside down or by one leg or even by their bills, as they feed. The impression of little parrots is strengthened by their short legs and the somewhat psittacine look of their strange bills; their habit of using beaks as aids in clambering about the trees does nothing to dispel the illusion.

Conifer seeds furnish a major proportion of their food but crossbills by no means restrict themselves to these. The buds in spring and later the seeds of other trees such as aspen and alder are part of the everyday diet, along with insects of many kinds. The homes of woolly aphids are picked apart and the inhabitants eaten; the larvae and pupae of moths are taken from their rolled-up leaf shelters or from wherever they have tried to conceal themselves. Even insects living in tree galls are not proof against the crossbills' powerful pincers, for the galls are sheared quickly in two to expose the creatures within. In addition to ordinary food, red crossbills apparently have a weakness for salt and salty substances. It leads them to some strange places, for A.C. Bent mentions their being seen around empty salt pork barrels in lumber camps and they come sometimes to the ashy remains of fires in quest of minerals.

Crossbills are given to periodic eruptions, quite apart from their erratic appearance and disappearance from certain areas. The seasons when these birds are especially numerous probably coincide with or follow times when conditions are unusually favourable for their breeding and proliferation.

Preceding the nest-building and egg-laying is a period of courtship with the male ritually feeding his mate and indulging in flight displays designed to win her affections and captivate her heart. From the tip of a conifer spire he launches into spread-tailed, stiff-winged flight that is accompanied by a prolonged outpouring of liquid song. There is also a song given from a perch, though it is shorter and less ecstatic than the one delivered in flight.

When the birds have paired the female begins building, putting together a nest of twigs, plant fibres, insect silk and *Usnea*, the hanging, greyish lichen. Bits of bark and decayed wood may be incorporated into the structure together with a few feathers in the lining. The nests are frequently placed in clumps of densely packed needles so that they are difficult to find. The height from the ground may be anywhere from ten to forty feet or more.

There are usually three or four chicks and from the time they hatch until they leave the nest to forage for themselves, the parents feed them on a regurgitated mixture of seeds. The female, too, is fed by her mate as long as she is incubating the eggs or brooding the young. Crossbills are not hatched with the peculiar mandibles of their kind but with conventional bills that change as the young mature. As the tips begin to cross they may twist to either left or right.

The first plumage is stripy and siskin-like but by the first winter it is succeeded in males by the patchy red and yellow shown in the painting. This unusual and rather lovely dress has all the beauty of a hardwood forest in fall: in it, in miniature, are exactly the flames, cherry reds and golds of an Adirondack ridge after the first October frost. When fully mature the males have a largely brick-red body plumage while at any stage of their lives females have no red but only shades of yellow.

Crossbills are great wanderers, going wherever food is plentiful and not having any regular form of migration. Our red crossbill and the bird of Europe and Asia are closely allied races which together with the white-winged species make up a group that is a part of the world's northern evergreen covering.

51 Oregon Junco

Junco hyemalis oreganus

As the robin is the messenger of spring's arrival east of the Rockies, so is the Oregon junco the herald of winter in the northwest. It comes with the first chill winds of late fall; the flash of its white tail feathers and the click and trill of its voice are sure signs that cold weather is on the way.

In southern British Columbia, in Washington and in Oregon, it is one of the most characteristic birds; it is the local race of a widespread, variable species now known as the dark-eyed junco. To townspeople seeing it appear around their houses, the junco signals the approach of winter, though on the Pacific coast it is not a migrant in any real sense. Come spring, juncos merely take up rural residence, returning to town after the breeding season to forage and flicker among the shrubs and dormant flower beds of parks and gardens.

In mid-winter, mixed with the blacks and cinnamons of this race, one may see an occasional monochrome charcoal form—a slate-coloured junco blown in on an arctic cold front from much farther north. It is an idle pastime of housebound days to watch the feeder for one of the "foreigners" and to speculate on the vagaries of weather and chance that brought it to the coast, far from its native northeast.

As the days lengthen and spring seems a possibility, the male juncos begin their simple song, ascending to the branches of small trees to utter a short, inflectionless melody. It is a weak, not unsweet trill, reminiscent of the chipping sparrow's song but less mechanical in quality.

The singing begins on fine days in early February and by March the juncos become scarcer and are seen less often in the suburbs. In parts of their range there is a definite migratory movement and in spring the birds move north, first to the lowlands and later to the higher altitudes where they spend the summer. However, in the northwest, at least in the part that I know, juncos move only a few miles out for the breeding season and one need only walk along a country road to see them darting and tail-fanning on the cleared edges of the forest.

The junco is a very familiar bird to me yet it is so associated in my mind with grey winter days that I feel an involuntary start of surprise whenever I flush one among the woodland salal on a summer day. From March until fall this is the home of the Oregon junco and where the young are raised. On the ground, in a hollow of moss, it builds its nest, forming the cup of dried grass and straws. The lining is of finer grass, perhaps intermingled with hair; the complete structure usually is concealed and protected by the fallen limb of a tree.

The brood of three or four grows quickly on a diet of caterpillars and other insects though the adults feed largely on a wide assortment of seeds. Almost all their food is gleaned from the ground, under bushes and in clearings, for these birds seldom go higher than low bushes.

Juncos enliven the days of winter with their trim, neat forms, their warm colours, staccato notes and lively actions. For us in the west, the wet, grey months of December and January would be greyer still without them.

52 Golden-crowned Sparrow

Zonotrichia atricapilla

The handsome golden-crowned sparrow is a bird only of the west and in particular of the land lying between the coast mountains and the Pacific shore. From the edge of the Arctic Circle to Baja, California it is plentiful, partly sharing its range with the closely related white-crowned sparrow. To some extent, these two species have different preferences in habitat but during migration time and in winter they come together and often can be seen in the same loose flocks.

Beginning in April, golden-crowned sparrows move north along the Pacific coast from the southern portion of their wintering grounds in California, appearing at points along the way in quite large numbers. According to a correspondent quoted in Bent's *Life Histories of North American Birds*, great flocks travel offshore, descending on and eating bare the vegetable gardens of island lightkeepers.

Golden-crowned sparrows have a fondness for edible greenery and will feed eagerly on newly-sprouted weeds, grass and cultivated vegetables. They like the tender buds of various trees and plants as well as the petals of flowers. This taste for flowers, fruit buds and garden produce makes them unpopular at times, for they can be destructive. It took me a long time to discover what it was that tore and shredded my crocus flowers each spring; I found it to be golden-crowns, though house sparrows, too, are guilty of the offence.

In the breeding season, golden-crowned sparrows go high and until September they are found on the coast-side slopes of the mountains right up to the timberline. There they frequent willow and alder stands and the dense vegetation of the canyons. Nests are built in the shelter of thickets, usually on the ground but sometimes a foot or two higher; there are always birds that do not conform to the rules. Though it is a commonly seen bird, not a great deal is known about this sparrow's courtship or of its behaviour at the nest. We do know that it builds a rather large nest composed of moss, grass, leaves and plant fibres.

Three to five eggs are laid and by the time of their departure the young are large, long-legged sparrows that closely resemble their parents, except for a more subdued head pattern. The adults lose, at least partially, the striking black markings on their crowns, having them replaced by narrower, streaky brown bands. As I write, I have in my hand an accidentally killed bird; it is November and this sparrow's crown and forehead are strongly suffused with yellow with a brown stripe running backward over each eye, ending in a few small streaks.

At this time, in the fall, we see them in the company of white-crowned sparrows wearing brown head stripes, and we must look fairly closely to separate the two. Golden-crowned sparrows are darker than the white-crowns and tend to remain closer to cover, venturing out in scattered groups to feed in the open.

On Vancouver Island, the most typical place to find them in winter is along country hedgerows that border fields. In the tangled, red-hipped wild rose and choke cherry little parties of six to a dozen "crowned" sparrows flit hurriedly from one clump of bushes to the protection of the next or sit taking the pale sunshine. Most of them are golden-crowns and from one or two comes an occasional, introspective song.

This song, plaintive and unmistakable, may be heard at any time of year, though in the off-season it may be incomplete or softly delivered. At its best, it consists of three descending notes in a minor key, quite unlike any other and easily imitated by whistling. Occasionally, the song ends in a trill and twice I have heard an even more elaborate version, remarkably like a white-crown's song. It was so similar that the close relationship between the species could be realized and the possible development of one song from the other understood. The golden-crowned sparrow has other notes, among them the metallic squeak that is most frequently heard.

This is a shy species that stays close to cover. In gardens and around houses it remains on the fringes of open spaces and the least alarm sends the flock fluttering up in jerky, long-tailed flight to the safety of surrounding bushes.

53 Fox Sparrow

Passerella iliaca

On the humid Pacific coast, "fox sparrow" seems inappropriate for this big, umber finch. Only its rump and tail are in any way "foxy" and they really are darker than any vulpine shade.

But the fox sparrow is wide-ranging and occurs in both eastern North America and in the west from the Alaskan tree line to California. It is like the song sparrow in showing tremendous variation in size and colouring in different parts of the continent. Ornithologists have divided it into a number of subspecies or races, all of which interbreed where they overlap and which are not always distinguishable in the field. The extreme forms are the eastern race and, darkest of all, that which breeds along the coast of British Columbia.

In the northwest we see large, dark sparrows, strongly spotted and streaked in rich browns. They are utterly different in appearance to eastern birds of the same species whose grey and bright rufous explains the name "fox sparrow."

The six or so races that concern us breed in Alaska, on the offshore islands and on the British Columbia coast. All spend the winter somewhere between these places and southern California and all travel down the west coast in fall. Those passing the summer farthest north move farthest south, leap-frogging migrants of more southerly breeding races that are content to spend the cold season in Washington and Oregon. Generally birds of ground-cover and the lowest undergrowth stratum, fox sparrows appear on migration in October and November, flying low in the night, resting and feeding by day.

In the fall of 1974, I walked into my garden and into the midst of a migration wave. The Garry oaks still held but a light wind had released the maple leaves, letting them drift down, huge and yellow, to carpet the grass and the tops of bushes. About me the clear bright air was vibrant with a contagious excitement; I felt the migrants' restless intensity. A winter wren worked hastily through the ivy, Audubon's warblers were in passage, golden-crowned sparrows called their distinctive note and the first juncos flicked from bush to bush. As I stood amid the small sounds, a party of fox sparrows blew in, alighted and began at once to scratch under the rhododendrons. Oblivious to my presence, they fed hurriedly, and their progress brought them to the leaf litter at my feet. I could discern their greyish faces and stout finch bills though it was not possible to tell their race. Certainly they had come from northern British Columbia or far up in Alaska; the lower mandibles showed corn yellow so perhaps they were birds of the Yakutat subspecies.

For a week or two we see them and then most pass by to California, leaving a few behind to remain for the winter. Bold in looks and size, nevertheless they come shyly to the feeder or hang back in the periphery with the more timid species. They are at any season retiring birds, preferring to remain in thick cover where they are difficult to glimpse.

Sometimes on their northward spring journey we are lucky enough to hear one sing its rich, sweet song from an elevated position. When the breeding grounds have been reached there will be several regularly visited song perches in each male's territory.

Fox sparrows are ground-nesters, laying three to five eggs in a structure tucked into a patch of moss or wedged in a sheltering crevice. The materials used are those lying readily to hand (or beak)—dry grass, leaves, moss and debris. The lining is of finer grass stems applied to the inner surface of the shell and shaped by the builder's body.

Like hermit thrushes, fox sparrows on their journeys seem to bump into things with distressing frequency. This may be due to their travelling near the ground at night but whatever the reason, I never fail to pick up several each season, victims of collision with power lines and windows.

Drawings

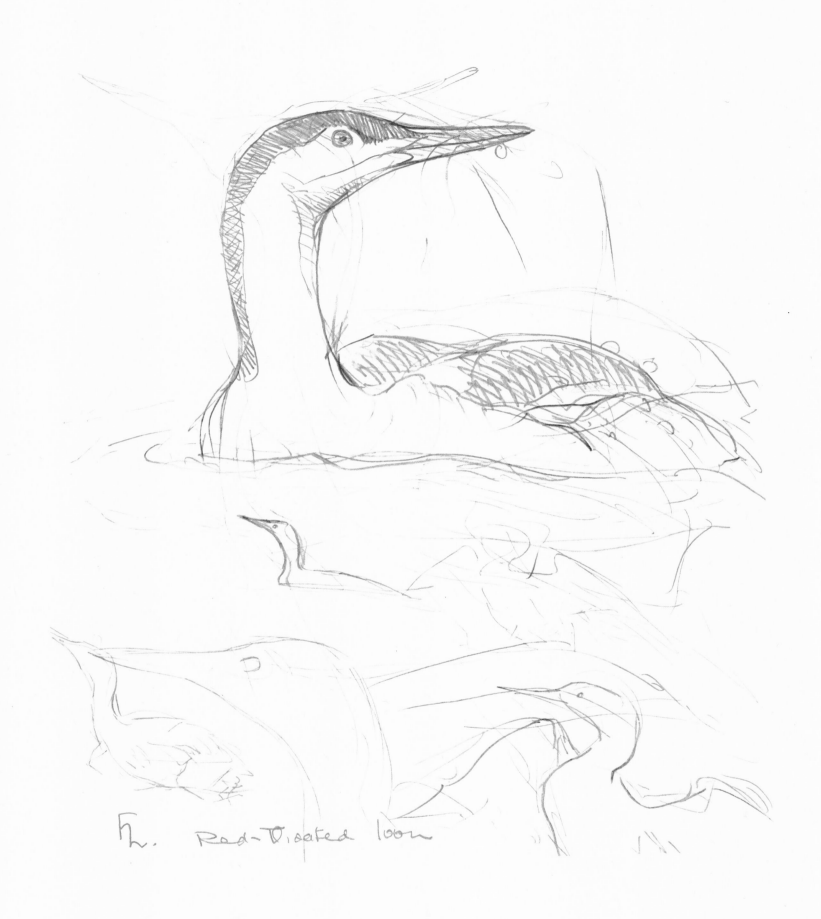

Red-throated loon

Horned grebe — winter

Brandt's Cormorant

Black.
Brant

Bufflehead

Harlequin ducks

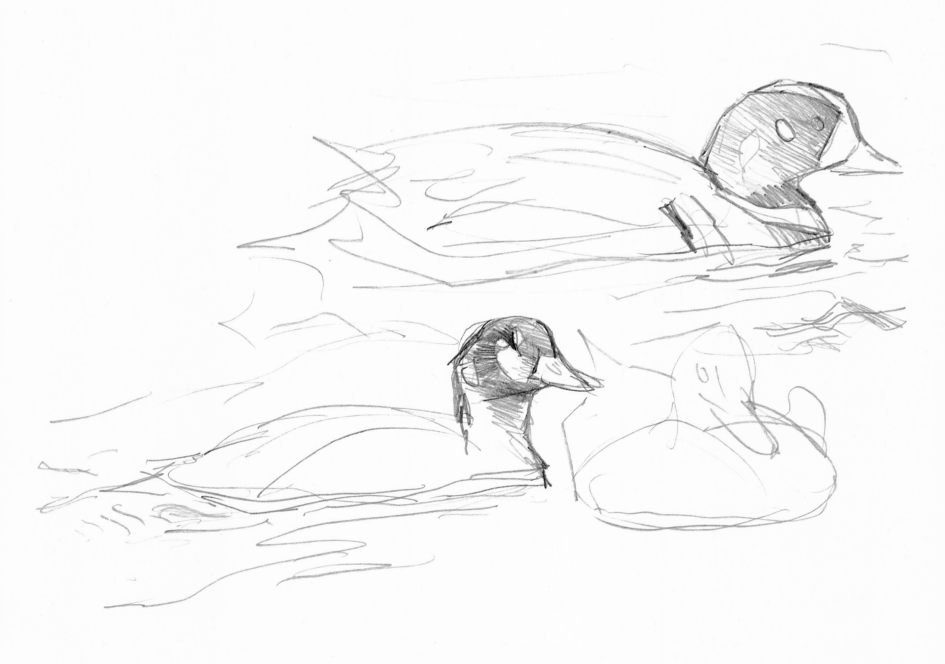

surf scoters

Cooper's Hawk
immature
FL

Red-tailed Hawk

Bald eagle – young bird
(2 yrs) with old squaw.

Sooty Grouse

Ruffed Grouse

California Quail

Black oystercatcher
Haematopus bachmani

Black Turnstones.

greater yellowlegs

Dunlin

F.L.

sanderling

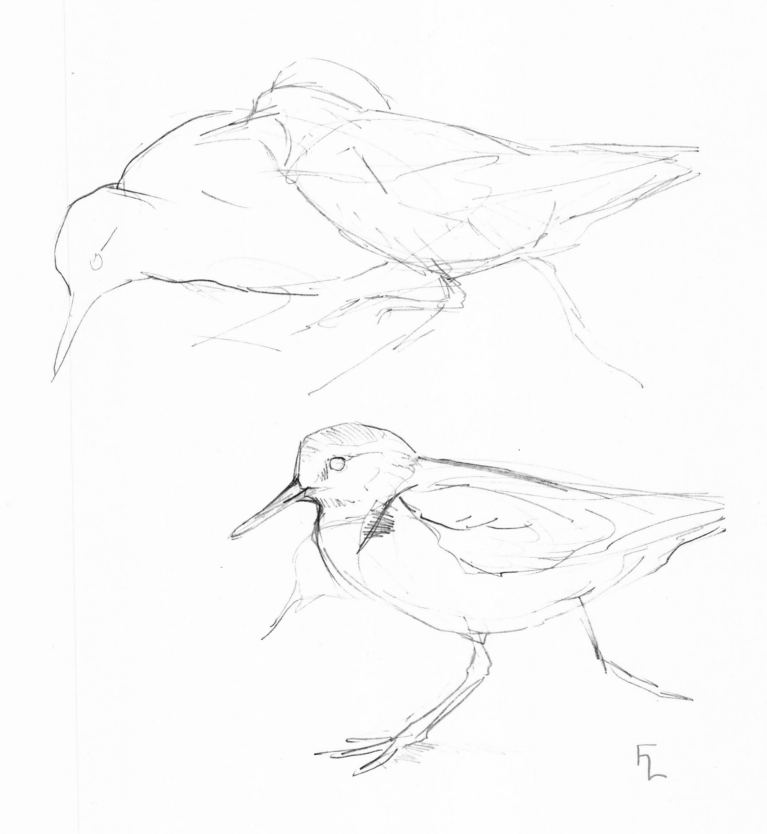

Glaucous winged gull.

Bonaparte's Gull

140

Common murre

Pigeon guillemot –
winter plumage.

F.

Marbled Murrelet

F.

Tufted Puffin

Band Tailed Pigeon

FL.

144

Snowy owl

F.

Pygmy owl with
junco

F.

Cape Vincent. N.Y.

Short-eared owl
dropping on prey
FL.

saw whet owl

Black swift.

fL

乙.

rufous hummer.

Common flicker

Red-breasted Sapsucker

western Flycatcher

F.

violet Green Swallow

F.

Steller's Jay 5.

Chestnut-backed chickadee —

Bewick's wren

Varied Thrush ♂
February 3rd, 1972.
Killed by hitting
a window.

Hermit Thrush

Hutton's Vireo

wilson's — tutescent warbler

Audubon's Warbler

Townsend's Warbler

male.

MacGillivray's warbler .

Brewer's blackbirds

western Tanager

male

FZ.

Black-headed Grosbeak ♀

red Crossbill

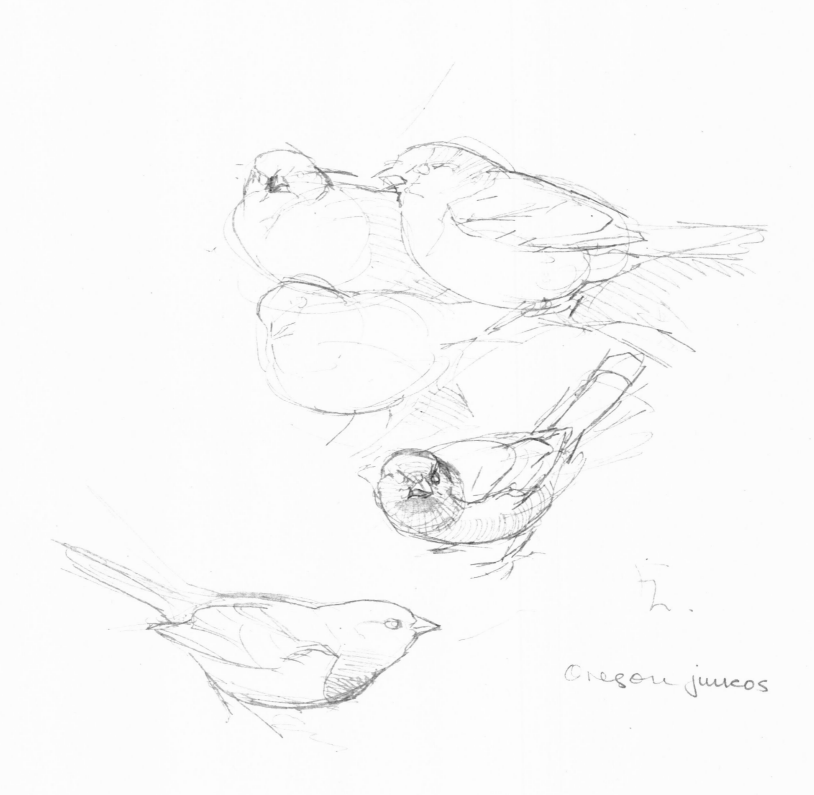

Oregon juncos

Golden-crowned
Sparrow.
February, 1972

Fox Sparrow -
Picked up dead, Victoria,
in October

List of Drawings

Bibliography and Index

Bibliography

AMERICAN ORNITHOLOGISTS' UNION, *Check-list of North American Birds* (5th edition). Baltimore: A.O.U., 1957.

AUDUBON, JOHN JAMES, *Ornithological Biographies*. Edinburgh: A. Black, Philadelphia: J. Dobson, 1837-1849.

BAKER, J.A., *The Peregrine*. New York: Harper and Row, 1967.

BENT, ARTHUR C., *Life Histories of North American Birds* (20 volumes). Washington: United States National Museum, 1919-1958.

FISHER, JAMES, *The Red Data Book*. Morges, Switzerland: International Union for the Conservation of Nature and Natural Resources, 1966.

FORBUSH, E.H, *and* MAY, JOHN B., *A Natural History of the Birds of Eastern and Central North America*. Boston: Houghton Mifflin Company, 1939.

GODFREY, W. EARL, *The Birds of Canada*. Ottawa: National Museum of Canada, 1966.

GRISCOM, L., *and* SPRUNT, A., *The Warblers of North America*. New York: The Devin-Adair Co., 1957.

KORTRIGHT, F.H., *Ducks, Geese and Swans of North America*. Washington: American Wildlife Institute, 1942.

LACK, DAVID, *Swifts in a Tower*. London: Methuen, 1956.

LIVINGSTON, J.A., *and* SINCLAIR, LISTER, *Darwin and the Galapagos*. Toronto: Canadian Broadcasting Corporation, 1966.

MUNRO, J.A, *and* COWAN, IAN MCTAGGART, *A Review of the Bird Fauna of British Columbia*. Victoria, B.C. Provincial Museum, Special Publication no. 2, 1947.

TAVERNER, P.A., *Birds of Canada*. Ottawa: Canadian Department of Mines Bulletin no. 72, 1934.

THORBURN, ARCHIBALD, *British Birds* (4 volumes). London: Longman, 1916.

WHITE, GILBERT, *Natural History of Selbourne*. New York: Dutton, 1972.

WILSON, ALEXANDER, *Wilson's American Ornithology*. New York: H.S. Samuels, 1853.

Index

Birds of the
West Coast
Volume One

Design: Howard Pain

Technical Consulting: Ernest Herzig

Editing: Dorothy Martins

Type was set in Canada by Computer Typesetting of
Canada. The book was printed and bound in Verona,
Italy, by Arnoldo Mondadori, Officine Grafiche.